AF244171

Once Bitten

ForEver

The Tree of Knowledge Of Good and Evil

William Thompson Jr

Dedication

To My Lord and Savior Jesus Christ; The
Almighty God,

The Everlasting Giver of Knowledge.
To the Beautiful Body of Believers; & to
My Fellow Laborers in the Gospel;

To My Family;
Thank You for your support through all
of my writing projects and endeavors.
The very best is yet to come!

Readers;
You Will Never Be The Same!

Contents

About The Author

William (Bill) Thompson Jr.

Has been in the ministry of preaching the gospel since Feb. 7,1982, and has engaged in studies and training of the bible. He has been in the church all of his natural life and has the experience of a true churchman that lends the passion for which he ministers the gospel of God. He is an ordained ministering elder of the Church since June 1998.

He attended the Fort Worth Independant School District and graduated from P. L. Dunbar Sr. High, class of 79'. He attended Tarrant County Junior College, Dallas Theological Seminary, and Vogue Beauty College.

His uncle; the late Apostle Russell Thompson, laid hands on him at the age of 11, from that point on he knew that there was more for him in the Lord.

He is a talented instrumentalist, and has composed many songs. Pastor Thompson has crossed the lines of denominational influences as a friend and brother, enabling himself to become identified as a child of God and not Just a Baptist, a Methodist, a Pentecostal, or as just another member of the Church Of God In Christ!

He is known and respected as a "True Prophet" of God. Pastor Thompson has been married to Sharon Renee for 25 years and is the father of four children.

Prologue

Tree of Knowledge;

of

Good and Evil*

And the Lord God took the man, and put him in the Garden of Eden to dress it and to keep it. And the Lord God commanded the man, saying, Of every tree of the garden thou mayest freely eat: But of the tree of the knowledge of good and evil, thou shalt not eat of it: for in the day that thou eatest thereof thou shalt surely die

GENESIS 2:15-17

The Entrance

HELLO; COME ON IN: the stage has been set, everything's in place for humanity, and of course the characters have all been named. The executive producer and screen writer has placed the script in the hands of the main players, and have rehearsed their parts.

This major life production and real dramatical scene takes place in the very true amphitheatre in the "Garden of Eden." This place has stirred much controversy over the years in and throughout the religious and scientific communities alike.

Many sociological groups arose to seek out and to find this originally configured prop which staged the entrance to the beginning of creation. Only they have not been able to actually locate the actual geographical location.

As a result, the reality of the garden, has been discounted altogether. I say; what a mighty God we serve! The only purpose, researchers would actually have for seeking the actual location of the garden, would be only for the reason of attempting to permanently undo the story of creation.

What's more amazing is everything that was created in the garden can all be found on the face of the earth today; with the exception to the two centered trees! It's not necessary to tread upon God's workstation as if to examine the tools that were used to make everything that was made.

The smarter people become as it relates to figuring out God and how He actually operates; the more spiritually illiterate and illogical they prove to be! While you might be looking for any particular land, let me encourage you to stop and drop down and start from the ground right there where you are; there you will find the beginning of your own existence!

Perhaps you scientific thinkers are actually telling the God of all creation that He does not even know where He started from the beginning to begin all that He had ever begun?

There has never been and there never will be a mind as creative as the masterful mind of the Creator, who stood from His own platform, and excellently spoke everything that He thought so beautifully into existence, which came forth just as brilliantly as He imagined it would, as He spoke it. The surety of His spoken creativeness affixed everything that was spoken into ever unchanging fixtures of immutable realities.

If we would be honest, even though we are spiritual, most of us are somewhat impressed with

Hollywood's film making at one point or another.

The film producers of Hollywood know how to imprint subliminal messages into the minds of the viewers of their films. The onscreen activities of the role players, many times, will have you spinning in your mind for weeks. The unbelievable stunts in the films are incredibly performed to create a believable scope of reality, when it is all only make believe.

On the other hand, everything that has been recorded in the written word of God, depicting the activities of the beginning in the garden, is all true! The role players are all real true to life players in the game of life. Not one thing has dissipated since the time of the garden, neither has anything that was; back at that time; changed, becoming something other than what it was at the time it was created.

Everything documented in the written word of God from the beginning has become a matter of permanent record. Most people only see the bible as a compilation of fragmented pieces of historical occurrences, but, I neglect not to inform you that the bible is one big picture! From the beginning to the end; or from the right side of the frame to the left side! Nevertheless, the total picture is complete!

The initializing event which took place in the garden, have even messed up the religious communities at large for any vast number of reasons for quite some time now. I have personally heard certain pastoral leaders arguing whether the forbidden fruit of the tree in midst of the garden was an apple? Even when corrected through the scripture, some of them still yet regress to teach the people of the church that the fruit was an apple.

God doesn't change ever! Had it been an apple that was forbidden back in the garden, the apple would even still be forbidden for mankind to eat. It doesn't matter how mankind bicker and throw tantrums over God's instructions, He meant what He said from the beginning.

The reason that man is in the trouble that they are in right now to this very day is for the reason of the fact that they always have a problem receiving whatever God said to be the truth.

Scene 1

Created, Commanded, Completed, Placed and Set the Tree of Knowledge In The Garden

And God said, Let the earth bring forth grass, the herb yielding seed, and the fruit tree yielding fruit after his kind, whose seed was in itself, and it was so. And the earth brought forth grass, and herb yielding seed after his kind, and the tree yielding fruit, whose seed was in itself, upon the earth: and God saw that it was good.

GENESIS 1:11-12

And out of the ground made the Lord God to grow every tree that is pleasant to the sight, and good for food; the tree of life also in the midst of the garden, and the tree of knowledge of good and evil. **GENESIS 2:9**

God; Told the Tree; To Be*

God; whose laboratory is within Him, drew up the blue prints of what would be known and referred to as a TREE with branches, leaves, and fruit, on the drawing board of His own immutable creative words.

God; so complete with everything at His disposal, that with the one word that it took to even speak the word tree, all textures of bark that would cover the outer layer of trees, the color for the leaves, and the color and meat texture of the fruit of every tree were also spoken into existence.

Every part of the tree above and beneath the surface of the ground were spoken into existence. The sap and the green filament of the leaves were put into place, for the nourishment and growth of the tree as well.

The very strength of the limbs for which men, primates and beasts would climb upon to reach protective heights above the earth away from predators; and most importantly to God; the seeds to reproduce after its own kind was also spoken into existence.

Of course from that point and time until now, trees even as they were created to be trees from the beginning are still trees. Trees are the largest of all plant life both upon the land and in the sea. Every tree serves its own purpose, and it has its own signature identification in terms of usage relative to the fruit of the trees and the wood that is used to build the homes and furniture that we use to enable our living.

I could go on and on to talk about trees in the natural sense for the purpose of educational entertainment, but it would be of no spiritual essence to you.

Firstly, I am neither a Botanist or a Biologist; therefore I am not scientifically prepared to submit comparative studies parallel to those who spend the balance of their time in the laboratory studying plant life.

I have not purposed to talk about a tree as a plant or natural resource, my intention is to discuss the purpose, position, and the promise of the "Tree of Knowledge of Good and Evil" in the midst of the garden.

This tree; creatively, though indeed spiritually spoken into existence, manifested in the natural, is so much more than what we could ever see with our natural eyes, or ever partake of for the sake of food or even for the purpose of

15

building furniture and houses. Our understandings are stopped at the actuality of the tree being wood substance, and entirely natural in all of the created realm of humanity.

Whatever the Lord instructed the tree to be or even not to be, it was so! Most people, that even believe the bible, don't usually express concern for the tree itself, as their interest is in the fact that the tree had something either on it or in it that did not fair too well for the benefit of mankind in light of man's disobedience.

The question is usually, why wasn't the tree or couldn't the tree have been more profitable for mankind whereas the fruit of it could have produced better circumstances?

The truth is that some people, even of this late generation, have never left the garden even though God drove Adam and Eve out of the garden and command them to live otherwise outwardly away from the garden, and He placed angels at each of the four corners of the garden to prevent them from ever entering the garden again.

So many people would love to reconstruct the events which took place in the midst of the garden. Most people being equally dissatisfied with both the fall of man in the garden where the first Adam failed us as mankind; and the perfect sacrifice of the second Adam; the quickening spirit, Jesus Christ; for what ever the reason they simply choose to disagree with the entire scenario.

Perhaps they would have preferred that God would have had nothing to do with the events which took place in the garden.

What many may be overlooking, is the events of the garden is the reason that people would even be enticed to take such negative positions towards the creator; being God!

It is so amazing to me that people seem to agree with the fact that water, plant life and trees preceded the coming of mankind or rather human-beings to the land, to inhabit and to dwell on the earth. Both scientist and Christians agree on that fact; science though, would rather wash God out the scenario, and totally discount the fact that is was God that created it all.

There is absolutely no way that God could be erased out of the beginning equation, because I've never seen a tree become anything other than a tree since I myself, have been alive on the earth.

There have been multiples of opportunities for trees to evolve into everything that science believes that a tree could become. If their theory were actually true and accurate, trees would not fail to transform themselves right before our very eyes.

In a human mind; carnally thinking in the flesh, it makes more sense that something would come out of something else, rather than for something actually being created out from nothing.

Naturally the potter would start with the clay to produce any desired effect created from the clay.

But what seems to slip the thought processing grip of the minds of many people is the fact that even the clay was created before any potter or scientist could ever discover it.

As mankind, because we are consistently digging to find or to discover knowledge and substance, it is often assumed that a discovery lends exclusivity to ownership as a result of the find.

Finding a particular thing (dis-cover) only bespeaks of the fact that a certain thing had already been previously concealed in an undisclosed place. So anyone with common sense would think to ask the question; "Who put it there?" How did the thing get there to begin with?

God being the one responsible for the thing found, and not only the find as the common denominator in either case scenario alleviates the possibility for the existence of pride, and negates the origination to claim human propriety.

Mankind found that trees would be good for quite a number of things; and we also discovered the fact that the fruit and nuts of the trees are very nutritious and beneficial for human growth and health. However, we were only allowed to find what God had already placed within our grasp!

The Command of God*

I am sold on the fact that God commanded everything that is upon the face of the earth, and yes that means me and you! In the very beginning God said; "LET THERE BE" and it is so even to this very day!

Perhaps you are scientifically affixed enough to think that you came from your parents; well consider the fact that the process of bringing you forth into the natural physical reality of your own personal being, is only because God commanded the man and the woman to be fruitful and to multiply.

That being said; not even your parents were their own parents and on and on all of the way back through their genealogical family tree. We are all out of Adam and Eve; since back to the beginning of time.

There is not a single tree standing in any forest, a park, on the roadside, in the yard of your home or any where in any country of the world that has always been there since the beginning of time.

But because of the "Genus" of the seed which was already in the tree and commanded to bring forth after its own kind; as the seeds fall to the earth they are positioned to bring forth other trees, and they have done so as they were commanded.

Let's not forget the fact that trees also serve the purpose of habitation for many of the animals in the wild in one way or another. Animals and insects also use the trees and the fruit of the trees for food and for survival.

Certain leaves of the trees are good medicine for animals. This could not be so just by the stroke of some kind of a freak happenstance of accidental natural cause. God planned it all from the beginning of creation. It is also possible that we as mankind have not discovered everything there is to know about the tree.

God's commandments are immutable: they are never capable of ever changing or of being altered in any way possible. God said it; and it is so!

Scene 2

The Seed of Knowledge**

And God said, let the earth bring forth grass, the herb yielding seed, and the fruit tree yielding fruit after his kind, whose seed is in itself, upon the earth: and it was so. And the earth brought forth grass, and the herb yielding seed after his kind, and the tree yielding fruit, whose seed was in itself, after his kind: and God saw that it was good.

Genesis 1:11-12

Seed -the source or the beginning of anything

****** *The seed is the continuation of everything living to reproduce after its own kind* (Author's definition)

Seed Ignition***

Remember that God created every herb, tree, and every natural food source with its seed inside of itself. In His infinite wisdom, God created the seed to ensure circulation in the continuation of the life cycle of everything that was created naturally in the earth. This is the reason that many of the very same duplicate natural plant sources can be found all over the planet, even in the seas. The message in every seed demands its space and the time of reoccurrence in all that would ever be declared a part of the truest process of nature.

God, being the maker and the creator of everything that was made in the earth, He knows the hidden characteristics as well as the displayed attributes of all that is visible to mankind. God specifically warned Adam of the consequences of touching and of even eating of this particular tree, as there could be explosive circumstances to follow. You must always remember that God told Adam from the very beginning that everything in the garden was created with its seed in itself. All that was created in the garden remains to this very day, as result of the seed inside of it.

Only the uniqueness in the reoccurring products of the trees in the midst of the garden were of a different source; the fruit of those two very special trees bore the hidden Eternal, Universal, and Everlasting seeds of a spiritual nature. It has not been written as to whether or not the seed inside of the fruit of the tree of knowledge were of visible, physical tangible characteristic in nature or not; but we do know that the fruit in fact of our biblical knowledge, bore a very powerful seed, indeed.

Had it not been for the fact that the seed of knowledge had already been strategically loaded inside of the tree in the midst of the garden from the beginning; the powerful duality in the productivity of knowledge could never have been released upon humanity within the atmospheric culture of learning for the rest of the natural existence of mankind. Knowledge, as exciting as it is, is both serenial and sinister; constructive and destructive; creative and cruel; altruistic and treacherous; etc......

It's as mysterious as it is also perplexing to the average human mind that the flesh of a natural colorful tasty fruit could be eaten; chewed, tasted, swallowed and even digested, but from now on the production of the seed of that same fruit would be spiritual and never ever again would it take on the physical natural attributes! The seeds from the tree of knowledge were never to be untimely released on humanity to reproduce trees after the similitude of its original design and structure, as of the created prototype in the midst of the garden, to further reproduce sinfully chaotic circumstances in the earth.

The one tree of the more eternal significance in which was also located right there in the midst of the garden, but was never allowed the chance to be touched, was known to be called; the "Tree of Life." This tree, that is later mentioned and found by the Crystal River in heaven, is said to bear twelve manners of fruit, whose leaves are good for the healing of the nations. What a tree! This tree bore the "Seeds of Eternal Life"; however since man was found to be sinful and untrustworthy, the seed of the tree could not be allowed to give the gift of "Eternity" to mankind, as was originally intended.

Jesus took the "Seeds of Eternal Life" upon Himself, and into His own prepared body, to redistribute them to humanity through the shedding of His own Blood on the cross of Calvary! Whereas the intended purpose of the "Seeds of Eternal Life" would never be forever lost to humanity, as a result of inquisitiveness to the point that they sinned. As the direct result of sin in the Garden of Eden, the seed of humanity was driven out of the garden and eventually distributed all over the face of the earth.

God told Adam to be fruitful and to multiply, and to replenish the earth; so we know that it was the original intention of God for the man that He created, to spread the seed of Humanity in the earth. However it doesn't take a rocket science for us as mankind to realize that it was also the

fault of man in that he was forced out of his own original habitat in the garden to make his own way in the earth, now unprotected and insecure of living, having had the relationship between man and God severed.

In past history many researchers have sought the location and the tree itself; but never successful in locating the geographical placement of the tree, nor the tree. It has been suggested that God perhaps had moved the tree, whereas it could never be found by sinful humanity ever again in the history of mankind on the face of the earth. As a matter of the fact, not even the Garden of Eden has ever been satisfactory located to this day. Much profound studies has determined that the garden's location was on the Continent of Africa; of which most of everything to be found on the earth can be found over in Africa.

John the Revelator; while in exile on the Isle of Patmos; during the translated exploration in which he was caught up into the Third Heaven, where he even reported that he saw things that were too wonderful to write; he locates the tree and gives description of the tree, so that we would later know of its location and eternal purpose. *Revelation 22:2*

The properties of this tree is good for the production of everlasting life; it has been revealed in the scripture that God drove Adam and Eve, from the garden lest they be tempted to eat of the "Tree of Life", and live forever! Alike the "Tree of Knowledge of Good and Evil" the focus has always been the fruit but, never the seed, of which the seed is what is responsible for the residual circumstantial influx and continual flow of knowledge in the realm of humanity, now forever.

The significant accounts of mankind in the Garden were of the more serious occurrences in our natural historical existence, for reason of the fact that these purported times were during the impacting ignition of every seed on the face of the planet. Personally I like to think of the seed as the very first computer chip on the face of the planet. The seed had the imputed knowledge inside of itself to reproduce what had been originally implanted, after its own kind without error or mistake.

Picture Perfect Seed**

We as human beings possibly may have been asking the wrong questions relative to the trees in the midst of the garden all along, for the simple reason that we are so prone to identify with the fruit of the trees though vaguely having respect of knowledgeable recognition for the seeds inside of the fruit. It is still the delight of the tasty fruit that we partake of as food sources. We know that the seeds of the delighted fruit for which we partake of are not to be ingested into our digestive systems. We have enough respect for seeds to know that they are to be replanted back into the ground.

For centuries now we have been focusing on the fruit of the trees in the midst of the garden, but now as of these later Millenniums and Centuries of the existence of humanity, we are victims of the autonomous powerful seed of Knowledge of Good and Evil.

Many years ago, whenever you walked into a grocery store over in the produce section of the store, there would also be a section there where you could buy seeds for planting your own garden, now of course things have changed and the purchases of seeds are not often found in grocery stores. The weightier significance in the package of seeds was the fact that there was never a picture of the seed, but rather a picture of the product that the seed would produce was placed on the cover of the package.

You will get the picture if you see it from this perspective; the scenery is there before the camera, even as the camera comes before the picture snap shot. Absolutely no one snaps a photo of nothing and get a beautiful photograph of the most wonderful anything! There has got to be an initially desired image to capture in the camera before ever taking the snap shot in the camera. God gave Adam the scenery in the garden, assuring him that every seed would produce the pictured snapshot in the natural, when planted. The snapshot is in the seed!

However, the devastation in the seed of knowledge, from the tree in the midst of the garden, was that the seed was possibly invisible in physical characteristics, but it would produce what would later be realized as being very present and visible in attributes, as result of the seed. They never felt the bulky firm seed lodging in their throats as it went down into their digestive system, but once the seed germinated and took root down on the inside of them, they knew that a seed had indeed been ingested inside of their bellies.

Every seed has the surrendered assurance that it is only going to reproduce the exact product of whatever it initially came out of, without failure or mistake! The seed is as sure as God who created it in the beginning of creation. No one has to ever tell the seed how to behave itself in the ground and neither does anyone have to ever tell the seed what to produce. As we are prone to listen to what the predetermined distinction of the seed has to say to us at the point of recognition, we soon see the truthful manifestation of the seeds that are sown in the ground.

I now know that it is fair for me to say to you that no seed is going to lie to you; it's going to bring the intended product of the seed for a truth, every time! What you see is what you get! You will never plant the seeds of a Rose bush, and get an Apple tree as a result. The intelligence of the seed is just too sophisticated, and accurate to produce after its own kind.

> *Be not deceived; God is not mocked: for whatsoever a man soweth, that shall he also reap. For he that soweth to his flesh shall of the flesh reap corruption; but he that soweth to the spirit shall of the spirit reap life everlasting. And let us not be weary in well doing; for in due season we shall reap if we faint not.*
> Galatians 6: 7-9

The profundity of this particular scripture, is all hinged on the truthful activity of eating from the tree in the midst of the garden, for which we would have never known the difference in contrast of sowing to the nature of the flesh, or to the spirit of God. The powerful release of the tree taught us that there were options to be explored, relative to our right of choice; whether the choices were to actually produce good or bad results for us.

Seed Continuum

It is not written in the scripture as to whether or not God ever showed Adam the seeds of every fruit, plant, herb, etc..., but we do know that He placed Adam in the midst of the Garden at a time of which everything in the garden was in full bloom, relative to what we know of as the

29

harvest time of fruit trees, nut trees, flowers and so on, respectively. It is always most important to know what every seed is going to produce, when planted in the ground.

The expectation of the exact seed that you planted can never be fouled, as the earth is given the ability to be on familiar terms with the impute of every seed, all alone without your help or assistance, the earth will yield to the direct command of the seed. The earth is of itself in direct communication with the hand of God, of which there is no way that God, could ever be duped!

Another area of focus has been the words spoken by God Himself, to Adam in the garden; "The very day that you eat of this fruit ye shall surely die!" What I have also come to realize is that death was truly attached to the seed of knowledge of good and evil, in that as a result of the hidden seed in the midst of the fruit, humanity have become very well acquainted with death. No one taught Cain to kill his own brother Abel; every knowledgeable scope of reasoning was passed down from Adam and Eve, to all humanity.

We of our own selfish nature as mankind, have always focused directly on our natural welfare which personally concerns us; we really prefer to live, and we are not at all fond of dying. We often wish that we could stop death and reverse this promised action in the midst of human existence, but because God said it; it is so! I often wonder why we have not sought after the reasoning for which God had given us this command.

The very moment that Adam partook of the fruit, God already knew it, as He is the one responsible for the seamless transfer of the seed from the fruit to the ground, for which the impact of growth is given. It is the hand of God which manipulated the earth into human existence; you should never forget the fact that God formed man from the dust of the earth; ground; whereas the actual seed of knowledge was implanted into *"human ground."* The seed of knowledge was planted, for which the process of growth was instantaneously ignited, whereas Adam and Eve began to know things that they had never known before. All of a sudden they were ashamed, fearful, confused and running scared from the voice of God in which they had greatly delighted in, initially!

I know that we are not completely accurate as to how long Adam and Eve walked around in the garden naked with no shame; because it wasn't dirty at that time to be naked! Every other created animal species, even to this very day, wear the true identity of their gender openly, and we have no shame when recognizing any male from a female in gender. God made us just like them originally, where we simply wore the identity of our gender openly; only we being made in the image and the likeness of God, we are the greatest beings in the earth for which the standards for being human, was to worship.

We knew spiritual intimacy with God our Father as mankind in the garden, whereas Adam and the Father were in a love affair under the cover of true relationship, for which any coverings of the human body in the natural was uncalled for. Now that Adam and Eve had become knowledgeable of sin and shame, until they realized the purpose of their own natural relationship as husband and wife, the worshipful nakedness between the two of them was to be concealed until the covenant of their relationship had been established to uncover the shamelessness of being naked before each other.

There was no such thing as a sexual scheme, for which one would expose their body to entice the sexual arousal of another individual. Knowledge; alone of itself told them to go and to hide themselves because they were naked, as if it was some sort of a revelation to God, even as if they needed to show Him respect or cover His eyes to protect Him from seeing something that He perhaps did not need to see.

Adam knew that God watched over them in the garden before eating the fruit, but after that one bite, the knowledgeable release told Adam the God was actually monitoring their behavior in the garden! Only; they had never misbehaved before having been beguiled by the serpent and Satan. In a since it was unnecessary to know the things to which they came to know in the garden, and even many of the things that we are so privy to as of now. Enquiry minds always want to know all things; as result, we have to ask God now, when at first because the relationship between God and man was untainted, God used to just tell the man whatever He wanted Him to know.

God was concern with the undetected exposure of the seed in the fruit for which man would never really be in control of the spread of the seed's product in the earth. Even though we think that we are in control of the knowledge that surrounds us, we have to admit that ever since that day back in the garden, that knowledge among humanity was forever unlocked! For that reason alone, no one on the face of the earth has a real monopoly on the acquisition of knowledge.

People by the scores expunge knowledge by the authority of their own will. You don't really have to be in a classroom to gain knowledge, especially in this vast, fast era of the computer. All it takes is a little discipline to apply oneself to sit down in front of the computer, or to open up a book and comprehensively read with the determination to understand the data. When your mind is made up absolutely no one can stop you!

Seed in the "*Root*"; In the Seed***

The purpose of the seed is to take root in

the earth, for which the root itself will receive the proper nourishment to grow out of the ground, further producing the initial product of the seed. The root is already in the seed; no matter of how long the seed is above the ground, even to the point of drying completely, the moment the seed has been planted in the ground and watered, the root of the product in the seed springs forth. Many seeds can remain capable of production over extended periods of time being left unplanted out of the ground. It takes both the water and the ground to ignite the growth of the planted seed.

Science has determined that the human body is consistent of 87% water; so whenever the seed was implanted into the human body, the seed was watered without being intentionally watered. Being an eternal seed; it has never been necessary for more seeds of knowledge to be implanted into the realm of humanity. Because the seed rooted inside of man, and as the root sprang forth into humanity, the roots attached themselves to the seed implementation of every fetus in the womb of the pregnant mother of a child.

This is the reason that children are born with natural propensities to do certain things without teaching and instruction; there is a certain knowledge that is applicable to every human being. The ability to know came from God in the beginning of creation, that above all things we would know our God and Creator. The ability to learn was released upon humanity the moment

that knowledge was also released upon humanity; as all that would be required to obtain the knowledge that had once been locked away in the tree, would be the ability to learn.

Ever learning, and never able to come to the knowledge of the truth.   II Timothy 3:7

Here in we see the reason that we are able to learn in classroom institutions and learning facilities until our brains burst with knowledge, but never come to the point of learning real truth, understanding the presence of God. We can never deny the fact that man has become knowledgeable of a lot of things, but, by the same token of knowledge, mankind is still at a loss for knowing the truth about the reality and truthful existence of God.

It's good and actually better to know God first; then afterwards, begin to apply acquired knowledge so that the knowledge can be filtered and purified. Remember that knowledge is both good and evil. Some good knowledge can be applied to an evil plot; like knowing where the bank is located, but only for the purpose of going there to rob the bank. Likewise, some people will attach a good cause to evil knowledge; the same way that drug dealers think of supporting the church with the blood money of drugs, murder, and theft.

Unless we allow God to help us with this

thing called knowledge, it can and will consume us. God helps us to get to the root of knowledge, before we wrongfully react on the knowledge to which we have acquired, without rightly calculating our response to what we have come to know. The untamed root of knowledge runs wildly ramped in and throughout the entire realm of humanity, directionless, aimlessly without a cause.

There are an estimated 4 Billion people or better on the face of the earth. Every one of these people have knowledge of one sort or another, by their own acquiescence, all they had to do was allow the knowledge to be lodged on the inside of their heads. Although most of us are very smart people, we all have to admit that there are many people who have the knowledge of things that we have never heard of our entire lives. There are even people who are learning things right now at this very moment that we have never even thought of learning, as we have no interest, or thought concerning those matters.

However, thank God, for Jesus Christ; we know God in the pardoning of our sins, and we have had our iniquities washed away, yet there are still many people who have the right to this same knowledge of God who are yet in limbo, and lacking the benefit of knowing God. Just imagine had the seed and the root of knowledge been released in its most purified state, whereas we would need but only to know God! What kind of a world would this world actually be!?

The contaminated root brought about the experiential knowledge of pain and suffering, devastation and destruction. Could you ever conceive in your mind the beauty of only having friends that would never become your enemies; or how about never having to work hard for a living as result of sin and iniquity?

What about living in a world that never needs hospitals or Mortuaries, simply because there would never have been any sickness or death because of sin which is the ultimate cause! Just imagine in your own mind, of never having to repent for doing wrong because we would have never learned to do the wrong thing; we would never even know what it means to be ashamed or to be convicted in our hearts, because we had failed God in our own chosen actions.

How wonderful it would have been to live in an eternal state of knowing, whereas learning would have never come into existence. My question to you today is; are you still learning, or do you know?

The process of learning is all a matter of time; it only takes a short period of time to actually learn a thing, and of course my friend it should never take you forever to acquire the information. Some people are rather inept of learning; they can't seem to hold on to the data once it has been given to them. There seems to be a wide gaping hole in their learning capacity.

Your inflated ego may keep you from ever knowing; just because you have become so overwhelmed with your ability to learn, you could become like others who feel that they have either learned all that they need to know or that they know all that they need to learn! Knowledge in and of itself is snake bitten, to the point that it is often poisoned; whereas it can actually prevent you from knowing the truth, leading you to think that you are still in learning, and in a quest for knowledge.

As a result of the free flow of knowledge, many have not accepted the things to which they themselves have come to know. I have found that many people are in constant question of everything that has infiltrated their own circle of life, which is the ultimate deception of the scheme of Satan from the beginning. Adam opened the window of the seed and allowed the snake bite to enter, leaving knowledge dangerously encumbered to mankind.

Scene 3

The Cost of Thought***

I verily thought with myself, that I ought to do many things contrary to the name of Jesus of Nazareth. Which thing I also did in Jerusalem: and many of the saints did I shut up in prison, having received authority from the chief priest; and when they were put to death, I gave my voice against them. And I punished them oft in every synagogue, and compelled them to blaspheme; and being exceedingly

mad against them, I persecuted them even unto strange cities. Whereupon as I went to Damascus with authority and commission from the chief priest, at midday, O king, I saw in the way a light from heaven, above the brightness of the sun, shinning round about me and them which journeyed with me. And when we were all fallen to the earth, I heard a voice speaking unto me, and saying in the Hebrew tongue, Saul, Saul, why persecutes thou me? It is hard for thee to kick against the pricks. And I said, who art thou Lord? And he said, I am Jesus whom thou persecutest. But rise, and stand upon thy feet: for I have appeared unto thee for this purpose, to make thee a minister and a witness both of these things which thou hast seen, and of those things of which I will appear unto thee; delivering thee from the people, and from the Gentiles, unto whom now I send thee, to open their eyes, and to turn them from darkness to light, and from the power of Satan unto God, that they may receive forgiveness of sins, and inheritance among them which are sanctified by faith that is in me.

The Acts 26: 9-18

Carried Away With Thought*

In the present society of which we live, we have over exaggerated the value of scholastic instructive educated thought, above and beyond that of passionately acquired wisdom through the

experience of learning while living through trial and error, failure and success, and the actual power of faith in God.

Almost never, are there celebrations that seem to award the justifiably substantiated excitement like that as of a graduation from an institution of learning, from our beginning early elementary education, clearly thru the collegiate graduate studies of our own chosen field of profession?

People, are awarded the highest certified recognition of accomplishments ever, for having completed years of expensive classroom education, even though some have been found to have cheated their way through testing and studies, never truly acquiring the supplied academics of study, which had indeed been obtained through financial investment?

They were even later found to be rather scholastically uninformed, and lacking the necessary knowledgebase information that would even qualify them as having being educated. The knowledge might have indeed reached their minds, but how to apply that which had been given to them as a way of living had not found its way to the forefront of their expensive thinking.

Of course, those people among us who have at least reported that they had attended collegiate schools of thought, on any level, having degreed documents of completion to show for their studies; they are usually more instantaneously considered to occupy the forefront positions of authority in our society, whether it has been found that they are even fully knowledgeable of their trade of skill or not?

As it relates to extended studies and higher education, it's past the time that we become aware of the fact that many people are losing the ability to discern the truth, even the truth of the knowledge that is acquired from their own courses of study, for the sake of being placed on pedal stools to be regarded as the better qualified individual for having paid the pricier financial sums for their own professional process of thought.

It is common to hear people talk of haven gone to college, even as they compare their institutional choice of learning with the others, thinking that they are better educated, as result of their own collegiate school of choice.

There are people, that are heaping to themselves, the kinds of teachers that shelve out unlimited hefty proportions of their own opinionated thoughts relative to the studies of the knowledge base topics that they teach, more so than the actual subject material itself? They are rather skillful at leaving the textbook information on the pages of the books. The actual literary data is assumed to have been read and studied to the point that the students are in agreement to the instructor's dialogue.

Most commonly, students suck up the

opinions of the knowledge, even more so than they actually expunge the given textbook knowledge, usually being a bit overwhelmed with the instructor. It is of our own natural propensities to want to know what the instructor thinks about the lessons that they are teaching, and sometimes the same questions are relative to the students; "What Do You Think About Us?"

We, of this present generation of people, are carried away with the potential of thought, more than ever in the history of mankind. Evolving technology is the sheer benefit of expanded knowledge, by which the minds of the better educated scientific explorers of the society are employed to consistently think on the betterment of living circumstances for the common wealth of humanity.

Back in the garden where all things were already revealed to Adam and Eve, by God; The intelligible blades of knowledge, released into the atmospheric realm of humanity from the tree of knowledge are as destructive, as they are beneficial to mankind, in that the knowledgeable data influx has severed its way into the process of thought and thinking;

Simply because we think it better to know for ourselves, without God's impute, people have allowed a deeper wedge to be driven between us and our God who made us, and created us to know and to apply the knowledge that we know, above and beyond that of every other created life form

43

on the face of the earth!

The tree in the midst of the Garden of Eden was called the tree of Knowledge of Good and Evil; why wasn't the tree called the "Tree of The Knowledge of the Truth?" Well I'm glad that you asked?

Knowledge, firstly and foremost only leads to the pathway that enables us to fine the truth, if and whenever we are seeking the truth, and willing to follow the pathway to the truth, which is the written word of God, that which is educationally acquired can be relegated as good knowledge.

Knowledge that pulls us in the opposite direction away from the knowledge of God, allows us to think of ourselves as being our own source of life, living, and of information, not needing to regard our creator as having been the one to implant the ability to process that knowledgeable imputation into our minds, in retrospect that knowledge in and of itself has to be reckoned as evil! All of the other grotesque deeds that are carried out in our daily lives are only the results of allowing our minds to become facilities that house evil data.

God; Himself; He is the truth! Adam and Eve already knew God exclusively, and they didn't have a need to know about any other knowledge of which would be later determined as good or evil! The knowledge of good and of evil would only prove to be necessary when mankind would

disobey the commandment of God, stepping away from the will of God.

As it is, whenever we step outside of the word and the will of God, it's the knowledge of good and evil that we need to establish the necessary boundaries to keep us at least living on track within the confines of human morality and the lawfulness of the land in which we live, being without the Holy Spirit to keep us in line with what is truly the righteousness of God. The knowledge of good and evil; readily avails itself at the breaking of each day, without desiring it to come, searching for the knowledge, or even the skill of the wisdom to know the difference between the two forces of good and evil!

Everybody knows the difference between good and evil, between right and wrong, between love and hate, and on, and on, etc... These particular contrasts of thinking and reality and understanding, were taught to us as children, even before we could truly understand the reasons for the diversity. Even a child between the age of 3-6 years, learns to recognize the difference between right and wrong, although we as parents are often in place to help them to establish the necessary boundaries for the benefit of their own behavior.

By all means, don't get me wrong; I do know the value of being swift of thought and accurate in decisive judgment, when dealing with the people of today in both business and in personal dealings. Illiteracy won't benefit the need to understand the phraseology and the implication of contracts, and business proposals, as what is needed most often at best, is the meeting of the minds. However, the dominance of thought and thinking, relative to being in control of the definitive comprehensiveness of the scriptures, can be the greatest hindrance to understanding the true meaning in the word of God.**

I am not talking about meditating on the word, which actually comes after haven mentally conceived the word, I'm talking about having the mind in progressive movement before reading ever takes place, whereas an aggressive idea of the mind concerning the word of God, is judgmentally affixed as a filter to ensure that the word of God doesn't alter the thought process of the mind in any way, as in the case of a mental barrier being erected in the mind before ever opening the pages of the bible.

When Respect of Thought Counts***

The relevance of expanded thought has its place all around us in every genre and on every platform. There is a noticeable difference between those who know and of those who simply do not! Only, the establishment of the placement of thoughts makes the biggest difference in the body of Christ, and even in life period! People consistently think on multiples of topical subject matter, but the thoughts that are being allowed to layer the minds of the average individual are often out of sync with the word of God.

Needing each other at one time or another, is a true thing of respect to be taken into consideration, but, total dependence on each other to develop our train of thought is a major handicap, as it relates to the body of Christ. However, even those who have been donned as masters of thought, they should not be relegated as being the authoritative permissive police of thought provocation, as they themselves are not always sure they have it right?

As a matter of the fact, most people are often found to be indigent of thought, as it relates to the word of God. In their determination to keep it simple, they often simply find themselves coming up short of the truest understanding intended for us to glean from the word of God.

Even great Scholastic thinkers find themselves often referring back to other renowned educated thinkers, relative to finding their way through the different facets of life. They say; "Great Minds Think Alike?"

Only, the danger of being mislead and perhaps being gravely misinformed lies amid the trusted interpreters of the thought matter, relative to these motivated thinkers. Many scholars have found that they themselves are at odds with what should be thought provoking material, and that they totally disagree with the trained pattern of thoughts and thinking of their instructors.

It is apparent to me that everyone that has set themselves down to study in a classroom, they are not all in the same frame of mind and thinking. People acquire information for many different reasons, for which they are not even in the least, conforming or even agreeable to one another. So to rely on another individual simply because they have acquired a college degree alike you are not at all as wise as one might believe.

In our own society, we have seen whereas people have acquired similar levels of study only to discover that one has learned for the sake of benefiting themselves in the society of which they are living; on the other hand, the other person has learned for the benefit of flattering a better criminal scheme in the very same society!

For an instance: we recently heard of the incredible criminal scheme of Bernie Madoff, of whom while supposedly serving the people of the society, he so under mindedly scammed the people and made off with their money! In the negative minds of criminals alike himself; he had a brilliant scheme. He scammed the people out of Fifty Billion Dollars; investment dollars vacuumed through the most unsuspecting window of

opportunity; retirement!

Whenever we begin looking to each other, the fact is that we never really know which of the two case scenarios we are being confronted with? Bernie Madoff; had the societal right face and collegiate background. The personal manipulation of the knowledge that he had acquired over the years, allowed him to slither right under the noses of the investing working class, supposedly upper-class, the more productively social class members of society.

Over a process of time, he learned to trust in the learned pattern of trickery to take that which never belonged to him and make it his. For quite a while his scam went undetected, even by those who have paid the greatest sums for being educated, and had been trusted and employed to front the top positions of the Corporations of the society. Even the paid better thinkers, you would think anyway; would fall prey to the low down scheme of one of its own members of trust.

If you were to visit the State or the Federal Penitentiary, you would not be able to distinguish just from looking upon the different individuals, who of them were truly graduates of higher learning institutions, as every one of the criminals in confinement are all adorned as convicted criminals. How smart are they really? Those persons behind bars only make up a fraction of the intelligent criminals who have been unleashed on the society, after graduating from a college

49

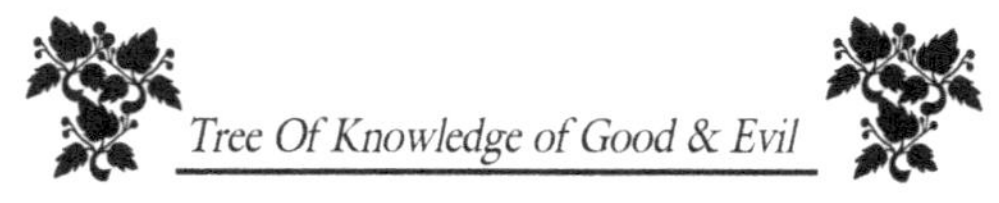

institute.

Many collegiate scholars, soon discover that those people who work with them, and those persons who are in close proximity to them on a daily basis, they do not always comprehend their dialogue. Often, laboratory experiments are conducted to establish the actual comprehensive levels of understanding among those who have given themselves to collegiate studies, to further determine whether or not those who have set themselves as students in the classrooms are being permanently effected to think relative to being educated.

Information Junkies***

For a truth, I have discovered that a vast majority of today's population are over-indulgers of information. Whether the information comes in the form of audio tapes, CDs, Video recordings, News Papers, Magazines, Books, E-Mails, Internet, and On-Line publications by all means people are giving themselves to it. This is the reason that we have so many reality shows and infomercials. Everywhere you go people want to know!

We have people by the scores now doing what is referred to as, comparative studies; whether in the churches, Theological Seminaries, Schools, Corporations, Manufacturers, Clearing Houses, Publishers, etc......... People are no longer

satisfied with the knowledge which they have already acquired. I'd like to give a new name to those people; I'll call them "Knowledge Checkers."

The foremost reason we have so much confusion in the world today is for the simple fact that people are no longer accepting of the knowledge, especially when it relates to the word of God, everybody needs a second and a third opinion.

The danger in refusing the enlightenment of spiritual revelation in the word of God is that it allowed for the differences between "Cross References" and "Comparative Studies" to be wrongfully fuse into becoming one and the same in meaningful relevance. The fact is that they are two totally different meanings of reference as it relates to studies. As a result most people who study the bible are all out of order and out of sync with the actual meanings in the written word of God.

Cross referencing, allows us to look across the pages of the written word of God, allowing us to stay on the inside of the Holy Bible, to connect a particular event, prophetic utterance which later manifested in biblical times, and even to strengthen biblical messages that are to be delivered to the body of Christ. While in cross reference of the scriptures, we often learn that the message of the bible has been the same from the beginning to the end of all bible writing.

Cross reference, should never put our minds

51

in opposition to other scholars of the same bible; and as a matter of the fact it doesn't! All of the prophets and the priests of the bible who knew the same God of Abraham, Isaac, and Jacob, their messages were parallel to one another; not contrary to one another's! So as we check the scripture by the way of other scripture, we soon discover that the message of the bible is clear.

Comparative studies, allows us to explore the entire religious spectrums of the world at large, having no boundaries. People of such studious behavior often find themselves seriously perplexed at the magnanimous volumes of contrastingly converse ideas which contradict the information to which they had first received! Comparative studies, as it relates to the word of God, is to the like of a wide-receiver on the football field who goes out for a long pass, possibly expecting to score a touchdown; but somehow the pass falls short of being received.

Of course, the pass rush is also strongly to be taken into consideration! Most people would never even think of such a thing as a knowledgeable pass rush, to hinder the knowledge from getting to them, but the fact is that the knowledge to which you may be gullibly gleaning, not knowing whether or not if it would even be beneficial or detrimental to you, comes with opposition.

In a game no matter of which side of the ball you are playing there is a time when during the game, the postural positions on the ball must change. Being carried away with the knowledge alone can at times hinder you from knowing when to switch your positions on the knowledge, or even when the direction of which the knowledge has come or to where it is actually flowing has shifted directions on you.

Leaping head first into pools of information having waves of knowledge without prayerful consideration can be to the likes of getting out on the game field, without the proper training and the skill to play the game. The greatest defeat is always right up under you, and even traveling with you all of the time. Pride; alike the serpent in the garden, is always hiding under the bush, or slithering out on a limb of the tree of knowledge to set you up for the biggest let down that you could ever experience in a life time.

Any wide-receiver should know that the defensive pass rush is not going to allow them to score at will if they have anything to do with it. Often times the ball is delivered just exactly as designed, but the defensive pass rush is also skilled to knock the ball down, and they often do. Whenever the receiver comes out of the huddle for the next play, they are aware that the opposition has also come out of the huddle as well.

Information junkies never bet on being literarily tackled out on the learning fields. Only, do we see the reoccurrence of believers downed, tackled, and seriously fouled while grasping for knowledge, in the church. This is so because, they have often become information junkies; they don't care where it comes from, or what the articles are that make up the knowledge, they just want to know! Every book about God other than the bible that hits the shelf in a book store, as long as it sounds interesting and intriguing to their mind, they buy it!

According to the ghetto jargon, junkies are those persons that are hooked on drugs usually? However, I have come to realize that we have people that are also hooked on finding and gorging themselves on knowledge! All kinds of knowledge! Of the most common, we find people arguing over what Jesus said; compared to what Elisha Mohammad said! These subjects have become somewhat even deadly among the Christian followers, and of those in which are follows of the Islamic religions. "Comparative Studies?"

I have found that those who have allowed themselves to become open minded believers, they have permitted their own minds to become vastly exploited! Not only are they allowing many thoughts of religious heresies to enter into their minds, but because of the open gates, they have also allowed the spiritual thoughts of the written word of God to be captured, and taken out of their heads. The solidarity of their thinking relative to God in Christ Jesus has been subtly sifted to the point that there is no more strength to

maintain the conviction of Christ's teachings anymore.

Many of the fellow clergymen, who study Theology from the much weakened boundary-less standpoints of Humanism' religious teachings, are often teaching the congregations now that the bible is too often taken out of context, whereas, a much less aggressive adherence to the bible would be sufficient in these latter times of which we are living! When the actual problem is that they themselves as the teachers of the bible have gullibly wandered intellectually outside of the contextual boundaries of the bible themselves, while studying.

So many of the now biblical Zealots have allowed their minds to wander into the secular fields of thought, whereas unparalleled patterns of thinking and thought have been erected to hold the written word of God under microscopic analysis, so to speak. No question about it, most everybody knows what the bible has to say about life and of living, but their curiosity has been stirred to the point that they want to know why the bible said it. They have further determined that the authority of the scripture should be thoroughly scrutinized.

They, who once believed the scriptures of the bible themselves, at the point of which they entered the seminary to study the bible to begin their search of the scriptural account of the written spiritual dialogue, have learned to

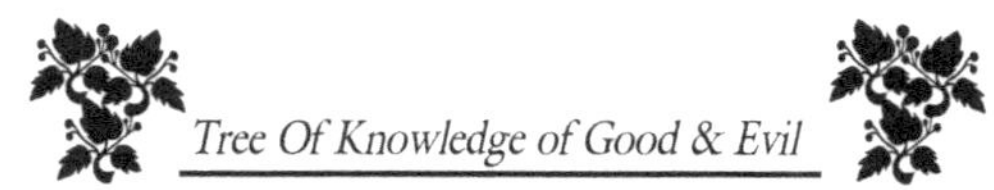

discredit their own beliefs. It amazes me, how that the people that are paying great sums to be trained to think according to the scripture, how they are taught not to take the bible too seriously, and they obey their teaching.

The unbelieving teaching instructor has got problems with the believing student/member of the church, who believe in the revelation of God's word. They have been taught to watch for and to develop problems with the people who have believed the word of God to the point that they have in fact taken the scriptural passages from the bible with them in prayer to gain a clearer and more profound understanding from the spirit of God.

What is often missed and overlooked, are the costs of disagreements among the teachers and the students in the body of Christ. There are not enough leaders today who are asking the questions, what is it going to cost the body of Christ if I teach in contrast to the written word of God?

Many deliverers of bible teachings are not even doing so for the benefit of the body of Christ at large; these paid information junkies are in competition to each other, to see who has acquired the more mind boggling, emotion jerking knowledge delivered in their sermons and bible lessons.

Back in the Garden of Eden, where the knowledge was first introduced to mankind, we

fell as a race of humanity on the face of the earth, from the once uninterrupted and unhindered relationship with God. Now that we are members of the body of Christ, since we have placed all knowledge over and above that of the Holy Scriptures, more and more, people are falling away from the faith of God, and even from the attendance of the churches.

America as a nation of people have fallen away from the once disciplined behavior of bible reading and spiritual devotion in the home. In many instances, the churches are even leaving the teachings of the bible to focus their thoughts for teaching, on the more societal issues that front the concerns of the community. Many of the churches' leaders have conformed to the rhetoric of the secular community in close proximity to their churches, they know that a greater majority of the people in the communities just around their churches do not even attend their worship services, whereas it also greatly assumed that they do not know the scripture and neither are interested in knowing what the scripture has to say about how they are living.

Most of today's church's leaders are thinking cost; they are thinking about the cost of what their thinking will accrue spiritually upon the church. As it appear that the economy has shrunken, they are also seeing the faithfulness of those who attend their churches begin to dwindle a bit. What has been affected in the churches

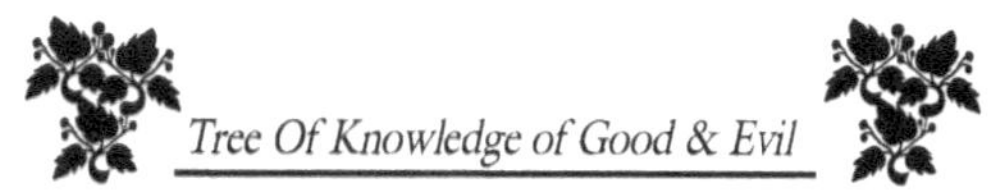

through the shrinking economy has not been the faith in God at all, but rather the money in the offering plate.

It is way too pricey to think of leaving the things of God, which is the only true reason that the church would turn to the things of the world, looking for schemes to keep the money coming into the church, to insure that the lifestyles of the rich and famous members of the clergy can be maintained.

You know what I mean; the churches have left off from conducting revival meetings that catered to the souls of men and women of the churches, to having conferences whereas classroom sessions are available for people to gain a knowledge to participate at higher levels in the forefront of the ministry, whether they have any business being in the position by way of the calling and of the anointing or not!

The churches are more interested in bringing in the finances in comparable rates to that of the higher corporations of the worlds. There is so much talk of the business end of the ministry now more than ever. What we have missed by the way of the deception of the enemy, is that it cost more money to consistently think about money in the churches. Didn't we hear the world say that you have got to spend money to make money?

What is the cost of what you are thinking?

Scene 4

Oh.; Now That We Know**

For I know that my redeemer liveth, and that he shall stand at the latter day upon the earth:

Job 19:25

My people are destroyed for lack of knowledge; because thou hast rejected knowledge, I will also reject thee, that thou shalt be no priest to me: seeing thou hast forgotten the law of thy God, I will also forget thy children.

Hosea 4:6

Thou knowest the commandments, Do not commit adultery, Do not kill, Do not steal, Do not bear false witness, Honour thy father and thy mother.

St. Matthew 18:20

That I may know him, and the power of his resurrection, and the fellowship of his sufferings, being made conformable unto his death;

Philippians 3:10

Ever learning, and never able to come to the knowledge of the truth.   II Timothy 3:7

Therefore to him that knoweth to do good, and doeth it not, to him it is sin.   James 4:17

We Continue To Know**

Satan promised Eve back in the garden, that we would know things; we have known good and evil since that day, though it has taken the spirit of the Lord to define the contrasting difference between the two. This might be a good time for me to say that it was never intended for Satan to ever give any instruction to mankind.

The scene of this traumatic infraction against mankind, just happen to take place at the same place that God had been giving instruction to the man in the first place! I often say; If only Adam had known that Satan was only an imitator, and a duplicator, with no natural propensities to be an originator, he probably would not have been apt to partake of the deception that had been handed to his wife.

Adam and Eve, actually ingested a whole lot more than they bit off, chewed up and swallowed. But, as I have stated before, it doesn't make since

to continue to hold Adam and Eve hostage for the same crime that has already been forgiven, and atoned. It is actually not what they did back in the garden that has got us as mankind in trouble with God, and the life that we are now living. The fact that we either ignore or fail to apply the knowledge that we have to our lives daily, is what get's us into trouble consistently.

It is to be known and respected of this present generation's Scholastical people, that from the very beginning, God is always in agreement with mankind having knowledge. In my own Para-phrasal commentary of Genesis; as God sat with Adam in the garden allowing him to give names to all of the animals, and to recognize trees, and the grass, water, mountains, and everything else that was available to him; God was filling him with knowledge.

As you study Genesis 2nd chapter, you will discover that God also gave instruction with the vast acquisition of knowledge, to the man. We error severely whenever we acquire knowledge without also receiving the applicable instruction for the knowledge that we have received. Common sense should bring us even to the understanding that when we acquire knowledge that we did not have already, that neither did we have the wherewithal to put the knowledge into the proper usage. We just didn't know!

Satan seduced mankind into making decisions for himself without being subject to God!

As a result of knowledge of all sorts, it is almost impossible to get people to understand that because Adam and Eve knew God exclusively, that they were in much better standing as created beings on the face of the earth. It is fair to say that Adam and Eve, were never aware of the fact that Satan would be setting them up for a universal fall as mankind, even for all of the ages to come.

We need to understand that they were rather excited to be introduced to something that they never had even heard of prior to the conversation with the serpent. Those of us who enjoy learning and acquiring new information, we have to admit that it is rather exciting to be taught things that we had never known before.

People that are really good at being taught, have to be very careful most of the times, because they often discover that they believe that they could do the job of the teacher? Some people allow their acquisition of knowledge to elevate their ego from being the student to the desire of being the teacher, after only a few classes of study. Suddenly the student may become unteachable, no longer feeling that they are in need of learning. They need to teach!

In my short life, I have come across some people that just made me want to vomit, they were so full of pride as a result of their intelligence, they thought? As long as we were speaking about Math, English, or Science; maybe even some other area of scholastic study, they were very taken with the conversation. But the moment that conversation turned in the direction of God, they showed on their faces that they were in total displeasure to the conversational dialogue.

Only God is to be on the throne: we are his workmanship; He knows what to do with us. We are never in control of Him! Although it is rather dethroning for us to allow the Lord to be first in our lives, please be advised that it is also of grave necessity to understand that our levels of knowledge is nowhere close to God; who created it all!

As knowledgeable, as many people are today, most people that I know, don't like being labeled a "know it all." There is absolutely nothing wrong with being very knowledgeable, other than the fact that knowledge should be revealed in our actions and our behavior, even in our choices.

While we as people squawk and complain about the quality of living and life, if we would really be honest, we will have to admit that we have not always applied the knowledge that we have acquired, to our practical living, everyday of our natural lives.

Lots of people are hung-up on knowing stuff! They feel that they are the most important persons who walk the planet, simply because they have acquired information of all sorts of data. Some people feel as if they are walking encyclopedias, dictionaries, and bibles. And of course, to talk to many of these persons, the vocabulary of their dialogue does often reveal that they have spent some time learning, and in studies.

I have personally been acquainted with a few people who have almost qualified themselves as a walking, talking instructional manual. They know how to tell you, or sometimes to even show you how everything is to be done. If for certain they cannot give you verbal or practicle instruction, they can certainly tell you that it is not being done right! Go Figure!

Any intelligent people will agree in acknowledgement, that knowledge is power, and often very powerful indeed! But, powerful knowledge indeed can also be as equally destructive; even in the very same mind that has been knowledgeably infused. In the minds of the wrong persons, knowledge can be very dangerous.

We are often admonished that what we know is not as important as pertaining to who it is that we know! While I do agree to a certain degree, I have to admit, that it is often what we truly know, that makes us who we are. Our knowledgeable base will often determine who we will choose to befriend.

Who we know can often be as damaging to us as the knowledge that we might have acquired that may have been wrong for us. Whether it is the knowledge and the acquaintance of bad

people, or the acquisition of bad data that we had stored into our minds; bad is bad!

Many arguments are made relative to what makes a bad person, bad? Are they really bad; or have they gotten hold of bad information, that corrupted their decisions, which might have spilled over into their behavior?

One thing I can say, is that they know something which either makes them who they are, or it effects who they are or should be! I am only speaking of the obvious, as it is often more easily detected when people are on their worse behavioral patterns of living. However, as we seek to find the solution for fixing the cited dysfunctions of mankind, it is necessary to realize that there is a driving factor behind the behavior of mankind, that causes them to come under certain categorical headings relative to the structure of their behavior.

Isn't it amazing that people are still being paid very hefty salaries for researching the behavioral patterns of other people? After all of this time, as people have come and gone, century after century, we still are in the need of finding the established rhythms of acquiring knowledge, and the application that place the mindset of most people on the forefront of societal questionnaires? We are still in need of knowing what it is that makes us all tick!

Along with the fact that people are consistently changing, day by day, and year after year; we have to also recognize the fact that people are always acquiring or either seeking to acquire more knowledge, whether the knowledge is that of Good or evil in nature.

Depending on who people are, and what it is that they are desiring to know, they really don't seem to be bothered about where it is that the knowledge comes from, or what it is that they have to do to acquire the rights to the knowledge. Many people will stop at nothing to actually be knowledgeable where others are not!

I have had some friends along the way that were so smart that they did even appear to really be normal. They were the people most referred to as nerds, and book worms! We often called them goofy! Others were definitely smarter than they even realized themselves. They were often in quest of more knowledge! They kept a book in their hands, and were always making themselves available to be present to hear certain speakers, as it would be desired that they might be further enlightened, and enhanced.

These were the people who never had a since of knowing that they had indeed run ahead of the crowd, so they continued to sprint for more knowledge. I need also to inform you of the fact that they also eventually blew out over the process of time, as a result of the data overload. Even computers will blow out as a result of the data over load. Too much, is too much! Do you know how much you can stand?

The Snake Is Still in The Midst Of Knowledge**

As we take a very practical look back into the story of the tree of Knowledge; we need to recognize that the snake is in the midst of the tree of Knowledge. The tree never came out of the snake; this would have suggested that knowledge in and of itself is evil, and that we as people of the Lord should shy away from any acquisition of knowledge.

The tree of Knowledge had been planted in the garden just as all of the other trees on the earth, by God. Therefore; it is intelligent for us to assess that knowledge came from God! Just as God put apples in the Apple tree, and Oranges in the Orange tree, God also put knowledge in the tree of Knowledge and the fruit thereof. God has never been afraid of mankind having knowledge, or being smart. God is in no way at all unintelligent or illiterate, nor indigent of understanding matter. God is responsible for it all!

Science is here on the earth for a purpose that should benefit mankind. Not for the purpose of erasing the reality of God or for reteaching mankind, so that we would forsake the reality of God; our own maker and creator. While Science does have its place among mankind, it doesn't stand along side God; as an equal entity for the welfare of mankind.

Science, in my own opinion, can only tell us how to use some of the things that have been given to us by the Lord. And in other instances, Science has to examine that that has been given to us by the Lord, to realize its function and purpose for being among us. Scientific findings, though, have often been found to be fallible, and incomplete; God is neither fallible or incomplete.

It is common practice for us to consider respectively the benefit of science and to equate Scientists as being smart people, even smarter than most people, simply because they spend most of their time in the laboratory applying their skills of learning and discovering even greater measures of acquiring information, to actually make men smarter and better informed.

Here: in my opinion; is where mankind have failed to realize that the snake had never left the presence of knowledge. Practicing Scientist have become so puffed up in their abilities to understand things through methods of applying equations that breakdown the compounded makeup of the thing; that they have begun to believe that they can define the origin and nature of God!

There is no documented origination of God; He never began because He always was and is and will always be! Likewise, God does not have

natural characteristics that would lend any truth to Scientific findings; God is a Spirit! So, while scientist persist to touch that which is entirely intangible to mankind, they are only further showing that they have indeed settled on snake bitten knowledge.

The snake keeps on whispering in the ears and in the spirits of mankind, telling them that they can acquire certain things through scientific measures, that are truly forever unattainable to mankind. It is just like the serpent to keep mankind preoccupied with trying to accomplish the types of things that are immaterial to any human accomplishment.

Just as the snake never left Eve alone in the garden to obey the commandments of God, and to discover the things that had been given to herself and to her husband, the snake continues to slither its way in around and through the branches of knowledge. We have got to realize that we have been left to handle snake bitten knowledge, as a result of snake infiltrated enticement to deceive Adam and Eve to touch and to taste the fruit of the forbidden tree of Knowledge.

We have got to also be willing to pass the knowledge that we acquire through the filter of the spirit of God, otherwise we leave ourselves vulnerable to the venomous snake bite, just waiting to happen in the spirit of our minds, and in the attitude of our emotions. People who acquire even good knowledge over a period of time, is still subject to begin to show unfavorable signs of pride and prejudice, as a result of knowing something that they never knew.

I would like to again borrow from the Mt. Sinai experience of Moses; as Moses approached the mountain side to witness the recorded burning bush; he also approached the mountain carrying a rod in his hand, of which bore two distinct characteristics that will lend credence to the subject matter.

First of all; the rod to which Moses was accustomed to have at his disposal, for every reason that I'm sure he could think of, was actually a severed limb from a tree which had been fashioned for use as a rod for the shepherd. Secondly; Moses had become quite knowledgeable in his use of the rod that he had in his hand as God enquired of the rod.

God in His infinite wisdom and sovereign spirit, He knows when we come before Him bearing whatever it is that we have been carrying around with us for extended periods of time. God knows that we feel knowledgeable about the things that we are carrying, being the only reason that we would even dare approach the presence of God with those things. You would have to know that we often feel most definitely to be in control over the things that are in our hands.

God says to Moses; what's that in your hand, Moses answers in confidence as he replies back

to God, already shaking at the sight of the burning bush; but hearing the voice of God speaking to him. God tells Moses to cast the rod down to the ground, and almost immediately the rod transforms into a snake.

Here's Why: God watched the man of God relying upon a severed piece of knowledge, for which he tended to his father-in-laws herd in the pasture. He evidently used the rod to find his way as he traveled through the wilderness. Remember Moses answered the Lord in confidence when he answered the Lord about the rod in his hand.

I always thought that the appearance of the snake was exclusively relative to gifts and callings, yet I still do believe that it *was*. But, I much better understand that the appearance of the snake was rather a sign to Moses and to humanity, of the fact that the knowledge that we acquire of our own cognizant ability, often bear the hidden influences of the snake, to puff us up, and lead us to a path that could be detrimental to our welfare, and even deadly, both naturally and spiritually, alike.

You should recall that I told you that God also gave the rules for applying the knowledge that Adam had received in the garden; here's God again, giving instruction to Moses relative to the knowledge that he had already acquired. God tells Moses to take up the rod after it had transformed into a snake, to take it by the tail! The hidden snake in knowledge always leads mankind to believe that they can handle the head of knowledge! The head of knowledge is God! He is the movement and the motion of knowledge that will have the tendency to move us sociably, financially, academically, spiritually and in every other necessary direction that we will ever need to be moved.

We know that snakes have movement and the ability to change the direction of their movement in a split second. The snake infiltrated influence of knowledge, will lead us to believe that knowledge alone of itself can move us around in life, taking us to platforms and to heights that are otherwise unattainable to mankind.

This is the reason that the side-winding influence of knowledge is so powerful in moving people from the otherwise platform base of having faith in God. Most people often feel so proud that they have accomplished a finished assignment of study, that it is almost impossible to stay grounded and refuse to become uplifted in pride. Many people actually become prideful, academically! They never intended to allow their intelligence to take them to a place of feeling superior to most others, and to the human cause for living.

Don't ever forget that it was Satan that influenced the snake in the first place! Satan was cast down, out of heaven, from the presence of God; because of pride. Genesis chapter 3; tells us that the serpent was already more subtle that any other creature in the garden. Satan, took advantage of the snakes subtlety and applied his extreme pride to that which never belonged to him in the first place. As of late, we need to take this very sinister relationship into serious consideration.

Satan, formed a coalition with the snake, of which I have never read that it had ever been reversed or changed. Satan knew, that if there would ever be a chance of getting on the inside of mankind, it would only be by way of knowledge through disobedience! And guess what? He's still getting in, on the inside of mankind all over the world through knowledge by way of disobedience and unbelief.

Satan, got Adam and Eve to disbelieve what they had already believed, as result of God's instructions to them. As of late we hear of people trying things that they otherwise had been led to believe that it was indeed wrong, according to the written word of God. The church has almost been transformed into being a worldly affair, relative to the behavior of the people that attend the worship services.

Science has made an attempt at reversing the seriousness of the written word of God; while society has taken a stab at altering the structure of worship in the churches. If we are not as prayerful and careful to be watchful of the influence of secular society, things are going to change right before our eyes, in ways that would only be pleasing to the devil!

The snake is still resting on the branches of knowledge; for the sake of those sadistic bible readers that have been looking for the spiritual positioning of the snake since the destructive encounter in the garden. Pay attention to people that are snake friendly, you will discover that they are prone to be people most opposed to the written word of God, in that they believe that forbidden areas of knowledge, better serve the causes of humanity.

For this reason alone, many people manufacture reading materials that are destructive to the readers who read the material. Knowledge alone is not at all righteous just being available for mankind to absolve into their own abilities to process thought, and to reason over matter.

> Because that, when they knew God, they glorifies him not as God, neither were thankful; but became vain in their imagination and their foolish heart was darkened. Professing themselves to be wise, they became fools, and changed the glory of the incorruptible God into an image made like to corruptible man, and to birds, and fourfooted beast, and creeping things.
>
> Romans 1:21-23

The danger of a Satanic infiltrated realm of knowledge and the ability to know things, is that all of a sudden, it was no longer God that men wanted to know. Men wouldn't be interested in knowing what God could do for them, they would be more interested in an attempt at fashioning a god that would be more obedient to them.

The one thing that God has always left available to us, has been the ability to know Him for who He is. There is not a limit as pertaining to the limit of the extent of a relationship that you can have with the Father, as a son of God. As long as we come before the Lord in the name of the only begotten Son Jesus Christ, we can have whatever we ask God for in faith, believing that He is!

The problem is that we want to know a *hocus-pocus* kind of god! One who will just give us things with no commitment of a relationship, with him. Most people want a god that is silent, unless or until they tell him to speak. So when many people come into contact with the one and the only wise God; they are not always as worshipful and thankful as they ought to be.

To be honest with you, I really can't imagine anyone being disappointed with God, after knowing who He is! To know God is to love Him; to love Him is to share Him with all humanity!

The only explanation that I will ever be able to offer for such twisted deception, would have to be that snake in the middle! If you really want to know God; you should be advised to check your motives and the intentions of your own heart.

Otherwise, the snake may be standing in the way of receiving, to offer an alternative to the almighty God! And as wise as you may believe that you are, you have no way around this ancient deception without God's eternal protection.

The angels bow down and worship Him before the throne, crying Holy, Holy, Holy! The angels of the Lord, are a quickening spirit. They can move about the entire universe quicker than you and I can bat an eye. Maybe you should even take into consideration of the fact that the angels of the Lord know for sure, the things that perhaps people alike yourself choose to doubt the true existence of. Everything that you and I cannot see in the spirit realm, they can see, and do see!

The angels have looked over into the pit of hell, and have heard the voice and commandment of God, telling Lucifer' and the fallen third part of the host of heaven, to be commended to the pit! Do you believe that the angels have any doubt to the existence of Heaven or Hell? The angels are spirits; smart men have convinced people to disbelieve that Heaven and Hell are real places.

I am not at all moved because others choose to disbelieve; those who choose to blot out the reality of God; Heaven and Hell; are generally people that would never be allowed to go to Heaven to live with the Lord in the first place. They blaspheme the Holy Ghost, and reject the truth of the word of God, and the deity of Christ.

There is no way that anyone is going to

heaven to be with the Father; who reject the only begotten Son, Jesus Christ. I'm not even going to let you come into my house, not even for a visit knowing that you hate my son! Jesus is dear to the Father; whether you like it or not, they are one!

You really need to know that there is no excuse for them that reject Jesus as Lord and Savior. Political correctness; wants us as believers to take down from the written fact that Jesus Christ is the only way to the Father, for the sake of Islamic believers, and Jewish believers who disbelieve more than they purport to believe. They just choose to exist, without any external connection of the natural realm.

Recently those of us who choose to believe the bible without compromise, are accused of being bullies, as it relates to our faithfulness to biblical requirements to live a Holy and separated in this present world, in Jesus Christ. It has been suggested that we should allow other Satanist and workers of witchcraft, voodoo, black magic, sorcery and all other types of demonically influenced rites into our worship services.

They have cited it not as being equal to all men, to preach that it is against God for them to live as wickedly as possible, while those of us in the body of Christ, live as Godly as possible. The snake has deceived them with the truth of the fact that God is for all people; truth! But, all people must come to the Father, through the Son Jesus

Christ, and repent and be cleansed and purged from the sinful stench of death, that reeks about their presence as long as they are indeed sin-full! When we persist to come before the Lord as sinful and wicked as possible with no desire for change, we set ourselves up as idols before him. God; is a jealous God! He will have no other gods before him!

He is jealous, and rightfully so! He is not sharing anything with any other being who decide that they deserve a piece of the action! Sinfully wicked people, have gotten tired of God actually being God, for the simple reason that God can never and will never ever change! He doesn't have a choice; there is no one else that He could ever be other than God; so you might as well get on with reverencing Him as God!

Now as touching things offered to idols, we know that we all have knowledge. Knowledge puffeth up, but charity edifieth. And if any man think that he knoweth anything, he knoweth nothing yet as he ought to know. But if any man love God, the same is known of him. As concerning therefore the eating of those things that are offered in sacrifice unto idols, we know that an idol is nothing in the world, and that there is none other God but one. For though there be that are called gods, whether in heaven or in earth, (as there be gods many, and lords many,) But to us there is but one God, the Father, of whom are all things, and we in him; and one Lord Jesus Christ, by whom are all things, and we by him. Howbeit there is not in every man that knowledge: for some with conscience of the idol unto this hour eat it as a thing offered unto an idol; and their conscience being weak is defiled. I Corinthians 8:1-7

The more we think that we know, the more we often think that we are. Many people have knighted themselves as the prince of their own ability to learn, and to retain that to which they have learned. In other words, they never give any credit to God for the ability to learn, citing the fact that there is people that are indeed incapable of learning. Some people are mentally incompetent, that have been that way from their birth.

For if a man think himself to be something, when he is nothing, he deceiveth himself.
Galatians 6:3

Is Knowing, Really Knowledge**

We all have the ability to know a lot of things that we were not actually knowledgeable of. Sort of to the likes of knowing of certain people that we have never been personally acquaintance with. We have never even been in their company for even ten minutes, to discover anything about their character.

Many people have heard of the story of the

79

garden of Eden; but they have never been made knowledgeably aware of the actual accounts relative to the scripture. Some people don't even know that the accounts of the scripture, took place in the book of Genesis. Just as most people know that the bible is the word of God, but they have never ever read it! As a matter of the fact, they purposefully stay away from reading the bible.

Most people are familiar, as well as mesmerized with magic, however, they are not knowledgeable at all when it come to performing the magic tricks. I can remember back in the early Seventies, when martial arts expert, Bruce Lee totally paralyzed the country with the extreme skill to perform his fighting techniques. We all know what we were able to see, but the knowledge to do what we saw was not available to us. Even to those who were somewhat trained in martial arts!

Well I know that you understand what I am conveying to you. As we acquire knowledge, it is imperative to be sure that we obtain the knowledge; in other words, we need to be sure that we get whatever we go after. Too often people are only being made aware of certain things to which they are never becoming intimately impregnable as the conduit for that particular knowledge. So many people are moving about in life, only knowing a lot of stuff, for which most of the things that they know; they are not even skilled to perform!

I know that what I've said reeks of being an oxymoron, but it is also the truthful reason that many things and people are out of control. Even many of the people who are indeed knowledgeable of the things that they are involved with on a daily basis, they need to rethink what they are thinking and to reexamine the knowledge that they possess again, in an effort to prevent the knowledge that they have from turning back on them like a snake, to levy a vicious bite to them.

We; at least, have got to know where the danger is in the midst of the knowledge to which we are acquiring. Here in is the danger of being gullible of knowledge alone. Many people have determined that they don't seem to need God, since they have been so successful at obtaining knowledge, and being privileged to progress much further in life as a result of having such extensive knowledge. People believe that they have mastered the art of living, as result of being so smart.

Nowadays, I even hear people make the argument that all people need is more knowledge and they will refrain from sinning against God. But I know, as well as many of you, that knowledge alone is not the answer to the problems that plague the souls of man, but to retain God in the knowledge, and to desire to acquire the knowledge of God, will aid in the behavioral changes of man.

O.K.; now that we know; we need to fill our

minds with God as well as the knowledge of God through His word.

To say it best, most people are satisfied with the spirit of knowledge alone, when we should be seeking to obtain spiritual knowledge. We now know where to look for the danger signs in knowledge. My purpose and intentions are not to pursue or to attack certain authors for their Godless literary works; but perhaps to speak to the people that continue to read those types of literature.

However, I have to start with the people who take the bible and turn it inside out, and upside down as a result of being so practical and smart; they think! The worst ministers are those who cannot reach the meat of the word of God, because they are so educated and theologically astute.

They place common since knowledge over spiritual revelation and spiritual enlightenment. The problem is that, there is nothing at all common about God, and neither is there anything common about the word of God that lends to understanding what has been written in the bible!

Whenever we settle for a common understanding, we miss God and the meaning in the written word of God. It is further required of us to bare down in study, while simultaneously attacking the fact that there are things in the word of God that we cannot seem to wrap our minds around, in prayer! If God can't tell us what

the meaning of the word is, it didn't come from
God.

Scene 5

Read Between the Lines

Ye are our epistle written in our hearts, known and read of all men: II Corinthians 3:2 *Of whom we have many things to say, and hard to be uttered, seeing ye are dull of hearing. For when for the time ye ought to be teachers, ye have need that one teach you again which be the first principles of the oracles of God; and are become such as have need of milk, and not of strong meat. For everyone that useth milk is unskillful in the word of righteousness: for he is a babe. But strong meat belongeth to them that are of full age, even those who by reason of use have their senses exercised to discern both good and evil.* Hebrews 6:11-14

There Is Strength In Reading Right

Judging the topical matter at hand, perhaps many people might debate that there are messages written between the lines of the scripture; and in between the lines of most reading materials in which we indulge ourselves.

Whether we are reading for the sake of entertainment, or for enlightenment, we should be determined to get to the bottom of everything there is to get out of our reading materials, even if, should we discover that there was actually nothing underneath the matter, to be brought to the forefront of our reasoning to be declared as informing and/or educating.

Most people who consider themselves to be avid readers, are often apt to give an enlightened overview that was gleaned from their own choice of reading materials; only though, I ask you to consider the fact that their reading choice of materials are often fictional or at least very secularly entertaining in its substance, entirely.

We have the presence of the whole make-believe genre which suggests travel in our minds to the secrete world of never-never-land, to excavate the buried treasures hidden beneath the chuckles, chagrins, and the laughs that tickled our fancies, to glean what should be the heightened

possibilities in essence for living.

Often the chosen materials are meaningless to the imminent welfare of mankind or to the intellectual enhancement of any reader that would even be interested in lending their undivided attention to those time consuming mind blocks, styled as entertainment reading.

As long as reading doesn't take us to the presence of God, or suggest that the righteousness of God be considered in every choice that we make, most professors and scholars often suggest that we allow our minds to open up completely and take uncharted explorations, whereas perhaps no human minds have ever wondered before? Wow! They say that's brilliant! Is It?.............

I've set across the table from certain people who could break down a sports article on an athlete, a coach, a team, a tournament series, or a particular athletic season, leaving the listeners of their conversations, to wonder why the writers left out the information that this individual had just divulged so meticulously?

They are so thorough in their discussion of the matters of the local news paper, it appears that they never miss an issue, or a detail in their choiced reading materials. They are willing to get underneath the articles to expose what the writer is saying in detail, or either what they might have omitted to say altogether.

Some people are as good or even better at discussing the articles of the news paper, just as the reporters and the editors alike, who created the articles. Being the author or the writer of certain articles of literature doesn't even matter, relative to those persons that have donned themselves as intellectual, literary analyst?

The danger of their discussions, is that they have the tendency to dissuade the readers that had been previously convinced; and to even persuade others that had not come to a point of decision concerning the reading materials, to accept the literary work as only an opinionated conglomeration of words.

Cleary, based upon their own convictions or the lack of convictions, they use their own authoritative propensities as analysts, to disavow the authenticity of the written truths in the reading materials, thus leaving other readers with discounted references of documentations, holding the material substances on the platform of questionable evaluation and examination.

They are often convinced that even as they themselves are unbelieving and shallow thinkers of most everything that they approach to read, that their only purpose is to disallow others the ability to see into the read materials, much deeper than the pages on which they had been written.

My friend you will find that there are more of these types of people among your own learning atmosphere, who are determined to convince you that it is not necessary to exegetically extract the

intense meaning and understanding necessary for practically applying the knowledge based information found in the word of God, to your behavioral patterns, to govern the manner of which you conduct yourself, relative to your own personal interactive standard of communicative involvement with others.

I have always been one to celebrate the intelligence of others, as a result I would inquire about their reading materials to hear their interpretation of the written story. I'm often intrigued as others go all the way out to put the message of the books into their own words. Although, it was not until they begin to tell me what they were indeed reading, that I realized that I was not at all interested in their choice of entertainment reading, at all.

Biblical readers, that are spiritually astute, who read for the revelatory comprehensive understanding, indulgent with the intent of getting to the meat of the word of God, the numbers are very few. The average bible readers are often grossly misguided to adhere to the opinions of the secular influences as they read, looking through the negatively obscured focal lenses of the ungodly, hindering them from seeing the need to read deeper into the read materials.

It is a grave miscarriage of judgment, to read the bible with the mental attitude of; what you see is what you get, and that's all that there is to receive from what you have read. I hear pastors and some teaching instructors suggest that they do not need to look to deeply into the word of God; they often prefer that we keep it simple!

I have come to realize that we are not actually involved in the subject matter at hand until we have cracked the invisible shell of the open spaces, between the lines of the paragraph!

The truth is that, most people don't even get to the meat of the story written on the original lines of the pages of the story! Most engage themselves to read with locked mentalities, closed understandings, and often they are grounded and weighted down with the preconceived ideas about life, which hampers their ability to even think sufficiently inside of their own boxed-in thinking capacity of which they are so accustomed to!

People approached the never ending depths in the word of God with their own shallow'd mental restraints; as a result, they are continuously in error to the word of God, lacking the ability to know the weightier matter in the word of the truth, which is God!

Life in and of itself often calls for stepping out, and thinking outside of the box. Many of us have been faced with challenges that have some how slipped through the gripping holds of the installed guidelines, that should have brought us to quick and conclusive solutions for the problems which had sprung forth from the unsuspected hiding places of life to knock us off of the track. But, to our surprise, the things that we automatically knew to do, somehow they failed us?

Those who have determined themselves to stay within the boundaries of the boxes, they have only discovered that they would have to deal with the disappointments of living for much longer that they would have had they taken the initiate to step outside of the box?

This would be an excellent place to make the mental note that stepping out never suggest that you step outside of the word of God! All of our help cometh from the Lord; don't allow your circumstances or any one that you may know to influence you to step away from the word of God for your solutions!

Being swayed from the urgent need to be diligently sober in our own thinking capacity while reading, leaves us to become readers that are indigent to comprehend the under-written message. We may even become dangerously influenced to be lookers, but never seerers; avid readers, but, never becoming able studiers? The written message of the bible, at face value, only otherwise unveils the cover in need of being pulled back from the laden bed with hidden messages right there in the middle of scriptural reading.

The very reason that many of the students

of our learning institutions are graduates but are not considered to be scholars; from early childhood development, to primary education and clearly through collegiate acquired professional degrees of career accomplishments, is because most of whom are basically become skilled readers, have never learned to study, much less to study what they have read. As life is passing by us fast, most people have learned to just make it, by the passing of time and life, doing just enough to keep up.

Back in the mid-to-late Seventies', the skill of speed reading was introduced to the general populous, whereas people by the scores learned to zoom through the pages of very large books, at a fraction of the time that it would take to normally read those books, and to comprehend what they had read. This was of course only part of the beginning of the era of which the American population would speed up and get in a hurry to acquire knowledge, and to live out loud; real fast!

So many people have discovered and have likewise determined that they have failed to get a thorough understanding of the life to which they are living. Many people have come to realize that they know a lot, but, not necessarily the practical application in the know how, to perform according to the knowledge in which they had acquired.

Too Much Interpretation; Not Enough Revelation*

Skimming across the top of the subject matter, takes much less time than it would if you were to dig in deeply seeking a thorough understanding, even in the presence of an extensive vocabulary knowledge. Words alone don't always lend the total comprehensive definition of the authors colloquial intent. Most often, it is actually what the author did not say; that actually lend the substance to what has indeed been stated on the pages.

Perhaps it's the omitted usage of the proper grammatical rules of writing that tells the story of what's been written? However, there are many rules of engagement, that may not necessarily be the quick pro-quo, as it relates to reading.

To the detriment of the general populous, most have learned to skim the pages of the book, and even most assuredly, the bible. While prioritizing, the things that are important to our lives are subsequently placed at the top of our agendas, of things to do, whereas we have confused the actual time that it takes to read through our reading materials,forcing us into the hurried frenzy of desperately acquiring knowledge because we think that we don't have much time to waist? What we will have read will often prove to be of no benefit to us, as a result of the data input that we will have overtly missed in our determination to swiftly skew the pages of our reading choices.

Now many English Majors, and Poetic Scholars would argue with me, vigorously challenging my assertion to the biblical relativity in the behavior of the average people of the church, in that they are usually lazy and inconsistent to go all of the way in studying the bible to get the total meaningful understanding from each of the 66 books of the bible.

If all were English Majors and Poets in the church, and of course, even in the world; the practice of reading between the lines, and studying beneath the surface as we open the book while looking at the pages, would indeed be a common practice.

However, even those who have become literarily astute would have to concur, that it is not the commonly typical practice in the average perusal of most written documents, to subjoin oneself to completely submerge, grasping the meaningful colloquy of their own reading choices, by actually getting underneath the embedded core to discover the secrets of the underlying interpretive dictum in the written dialogue.

Most biblical students are vigorously challenged not to become too exegetical of the scripture; as it is often preferred that the bible be read relative to historical accounts that may be outdated for our present generations?

Back in High school, the upper English, History, and the Drama classes were of the more defining courses of study, in that those who fared well in those courses were often thought of as the more intellectual students in the school. Here's Why: As we studied the Shakespearean Themes, and the literary works of historical Poetic authors, we were encouraged to develop the intuitive skills of our own thought process, for the benefit of breaking down satirical compositions, and the sarcastic babble intermingled with the story-line, written primarily, only for the intent to intrigue the very process of thought and of thinking alike.

I, for one, have become rather critical of the more scholastically indulged persons around the church, who place knowledge and the actuality of knowing above the acquisition of faith, which requires anyone to believe firstly to establish the parameters of obedience for the benefit of eventually seeing what is expected; they tend to be negatively analytical of the scripture, from the standpoint of disbelieving that the bible is even the word of God. Skeptical people, have a way of blocking and hindering the move of the spirit of the Lord in the worship services. They share their feelings of disbelief and the development of their unbelieving attitude, with all of the people of the church that will listen to their hopeless reasoning.

We need less of these types of people up front in the ministries of the churches, that

95

actually block the possibilities of the people becoming acquainted with the powerful movement of the spirit of the Lord in the lives of the people of the church. Such acquaintances with God, start firstly with searching the scriptures, seeking for an understanding of the reality of God, so that the actuality of a relationship with God can be realized.

Doubters, and the unbelievers themselves, are actually in the spiritual and the psychological state that they're in, simply because they have chosen to act upon the conclusive reasoning of their own fearful minds, though biblically inconclusive; of not trusting in God, and the word of God by faith, believing to eventually see! True faith in God, involves trusting in Him righteously, giving Him the total control of your thought process, from the standpoint that God, and the word of God are given total consideration upon your initial thoughts, decisions, and your actions.

I am not speaking in reference to thinking about God and the word of God, before going ahead to do whatever we have chosen to do, even though our choice of behavior is going to transgress the laws of God's word.

Too many people have dangerously placed their own minds over and above the knowledge of God. They believe that their own intuition has more power than the spirit of the Lord. A true fact is that, many people have taken the notion to think for themselves; however, they are consistently out of the proper context of thinking, relationally towards the word of God.

As the average person would like to believe that their mind is very sharp, and that their IQ is above average; most have failed to realize the deceptiveness of their own minds, in that they have allowed themselves to think that they know what's best for themselves, better than God, who made us all!

Just because we are quite accomplished in the development skills of our ability to learn, doesn't mean that we have been given the rights to personally interpret the word of God for ourselves! Several people feel that they are smart and that they don't need any unseen spirit to mysteriously reveal the meaning of the bible to them. They prefer the local library above going down on their knees to hear from God. It's all about being in control relative to what they are willing to hear. They don't mind hearing about God, whether in a book other than the bible, or by way of some instructor in a classroom, on a tape, CD, or other forms of media transmission on a computer.

It's been my observation, that the people of the churches of today are simply not interested in hearing the voice of God for themselves? Much erroneous teaching have been allowed across the pulpits of the churches, in every denomination? People who feel good about themselves, and have allowed others to stroke their egos, have stepped up forward to take the helm of the leadership in the churches, though they have no relationship with God; and even though they have never been called of God to lead the church.

They are often guilty of allowing their feelings and their emotions to dictate to them what they feel that the word of God is saying to them? As a result, they spread the same erroneous interpretations of their own sometimes heartfelt thinking, to the people in the congregation of their churches.

Many will even misinterpret a dream that they have had, suggesting that the dream came to them as a result of looking into the word of God, only when searching the scripture properly and thoroughly, it has been later discovered that their interpretation of the dream was all wrong.

However, some are so bold in their decision to interpret the meaning of their own dreams for themselves, though they have never been gifted of the spirit of the Lord to do so, that they will never even go back to the word of God to be sure that they were right in their initial determination to share their own intuitive conception with the people of the church.

No matter what you say to them, or even how you might go about making an attempt to show them in the word of God that they were indeed in error in their own understanding, they are not going to be told that they were wrong in any way!

My friend, far too many people have learned to celebrate their own minds, and their ability to think for themselves, over and above truly worshiping God, who is the author and the finisher of our faith! Thinking is a viable tool and it can be a powerful weapon against the enemy of our mind; and in our minds; but, our own personal thinking capacity should never be erected as our own choice of leadership over and above that of the Spirit; and the word of God!

> *And be not conformed to this world: but be ye transformed by the renewing of your mind, that ye may prove what is that good, and acceptable, and perfect, will of God.*   Romans 12:2

Even thinking, alone of itself; according to the word of God, cannot cause a man to change his ways, but his own mind has to be renewed by the power of the Holy Ghost, in an effort for him to begin to think differently on a consistent basis. As a result, the actions of the man will also be altered for as long as he remains in the different train of thinking.

As intelligent as we are as human beings, at best, what we know is the recognition of the feelings and the emotions that we have, and we learn how to react accordingly to the feelings and emotions. But with that being said, our smart minds don't always allow us as humans to control the feelings and the emotions that we do have; if so, there would not be so many people depressed and suicidal, confused about their gender and sexual preferences, and totally perplexed and disenchanted about the very next moment of their coming lives. We get so carried away with knowing the things that we do know, that we often fail to recognize the things that we don't know, and to take inventory of the knowledge that we need to acquire.

I have personally realized, that the more I learn, it means; the more there is to be learned! It's not possible to gain all of the knowledge there is to be acquired, as a single individual. This is the reason that a corporation has so many people to successfully run the company! One mind does not make a corporation! Everybody is given a different job to do, and that is not relative to the time factor of each job performance alone? Every mind has to think simultaneously, though skillfully accurate, on a different area of the corporate business, in order to put a different piece of the puzzle together with the other pieces, so that the big picture is clearly realized. God has ordained that each person would do their part to collectively produce the desired reality of the corporate thought.

Reading In The Dark***

   A well lit room does not necessarily

constitute that we are reading the word of God in the light! Lots of people gaze into the pages of the bible under the florescent highlight of a lamp, or some other specified light for reading, which may also have magnifying capabilities, but the external atmospheric surroundings have no bearings on the internal darkness which blankets the individual's mind's eye, and causes spiritual blindness and sinful affixation.

Sin covers and darkens the reasoning of the mind, in that it disallows an individual from clearly seeing the fault line which lies beneath their own skin; in their own mindset, and even in their own heart, driving them and further conditioning them to remain in the sinful state! The actuality of sin in our lives, places us in an embarrassing state, to the point that we are forced to look at our selves in the mirrors of morality, only to realize that what we might have participated in, in our natural bodies has indeed been unrighteous, and transgression to the word of God.

Having sinned alone, does not make for total darkness of which one might have found themselves in; simply because the grace of God through repentance, has provided a remedy for sin. However, as people fail to even acknowledge that their behavior is sinful, based on the feelings of their actual physical indulgence of sin, and further determining to continue in the way of their sinfulness, the light of their own mind, if there had ever been any light, will have indeed been extinguished.

People place themselves in the shadow of the darkness of this world willfully choosing to disobey the word of God. I have had so many people to tell me that people don't live by the bible any more, as if that was some sort of a news flash to me! I only observed some of those same people, sitting with a bible in their hand, reading it with the intentions of sharing it with others, although they themselves are determined to live outlandishly in error to the word of God.

Lots of people believe that a revelation in their own mind will turn the light on for themselves and for others to see? The only problem is that, the spirit of darkness on the inside of those individuals, is what is supposedly shinning an illumination on their understanding, but be advised, it is definitely not the light! Far too many people are willing to accept an illumination of any sort, because they refuse to come face to face with the sin in their lives, to rectify the situations of sin selfishness, before God!

It doesn't really matter how long and how often you look into the word of God, looking from the perspective of the darkness of your own understanding, you will never know for a truth that you had missed the truth in the word of God until you first come to the light! You will find that it was not at all necessary to try and spread

your sins all over the mercy Jesus; in retrospect, all you needed to do, was to allow the name, and the blood of Jesus to be completely spread all over your sins!

People that are truly of the darkness, are often found attempting to shift the blame of their own sinfulness on the Lord. The try to foolishly back God in a corner with His own word, as if God can be punked! Though you may truly desire to come out from beneath the bondage to the sinfulness of your own lifestyle, you are going to have to do things God's way, and come to the light!

Before you can see the word of God, from the standpoint of being able to break it off into the lives of others, you must first see the dissipation of the darkness that both blankets your mind, and embodies your choice of living. You have got to be sure that the darkness that once covered your own heart, that it has been totally removed, allowing the transforming, overcoming power of the word of God to have free course in your life.

Darkness is a barrier; it stops movement, it clogs the understanding of the mentality, it hinders the ability to grow, and stagnates the life of everything living? Many who have made public confession in the churches, have made darkened confessions, simply because they were never determined to be changed!

People have been fooled into believing that

God ought to just do it anyway, whether they change their ways or not! There is more at stake than just you whenever you come to the Lord to be changed? Consider the generations before you were even thought of, who came out of the darkness into the marvelous light of the Lord! They had to do it, and so do you! God don't work in the dark, and He doesn't apologize!

> *And this is the condemnation, that light is come into the world, and men loved darkness rather than light, because their deeds were evil. For everyone that doeth evil hatheth the light, neither cometh to the light, lest his deeds should be reproved. But he that doeth truth cometh to the light, that his deeds may be made manifest, that they are wrought in God.*
>
> St. John 3:19-21
>
> *For God, who commanded the light to shine out of darkness, hath shined in our hearts, to give the light of the knowledge of the glory of God in the face of Jesus Christ.*
>
> II Corinthians 4:6

Don't be fooled, light is definitely a God thing! Even from the binning of the creation, God released the glory of light upon the face of the formless, lifeless earth, to begin creating. He could have done it from the dark but thank God that he didn't do it! Had God created us in the dark, we would have never known who we are, even to this

very day!

So, to remain under the blanket of darkness in our own sinful minds, is to suggest that we are determined never to see the truth! The light allows us to see the revelation of God's word!

The same revealing power needed to enable us to read between the lines of living, life and the word of God, is found only in the light of God; in Christ Jesus! As the root of the tree of knowledge is yet in the throat of mankind, as a result of haven bitten the forbidden fruit of the tree of knowledge, the availability of knowledge itself often flee our grasp to understand.

Scene 6

Are You Really Smart?

And the Lord answedred me and said, Write the vision, and make it plain upon tables, that he may run that readeth it. For the vision is yet for an appointed time, but at the end it shall speak, and not lie: because it will surely come, it will not tarry.

Habakkuk 2:2-3

Educated; But! Unlearned

Many people have spent anywhere from 4-12 years, and maybe even more years of study in college and in higher learning institutions further educating themselves, who consequently, have never even worked or applied their schooling to financially support themselves since being educated. How smart is that? Most have gone into alternative fields of employment to earn their financial support for a living.

I have met people by the scores who have literally become human canisters and information file cabinets, but they are often too disinterested in their own chosen field of study to apply their learning to change the living conditions in their own personal surrounding, and communities. Some have even communicated to me that they prefer to keep it confidential that they had been thoroughly educated.

Their own living conditions are substandard, and definitely below their own desired expectations. They prefer employment with income inadequate to produce the baseline support necessary for the transformation of living, to mirror that they had energetically put forth the time to acquire the knowledge base skills of trade, to move from where they are, to where they always desired to be.

Although people are intellectually educated now, they still have the ability to find the explanations applicable to the excuses that they choose to offer as a reason for haven chosen to sit on the wealth of information to which they have acquired over the past years. The knowledge of their past experiences of life and of living, have actually padlocked their ability to learn a better way of living, beyond the painfully negative streams of reality to which they had been so accustom to.

Psychologically, life and living is extremely difficult; some people have convinced themselves that the dreams bouncing around and abounding in their heads are forever impossible to realize. Although they graduated from institutes of knowledgeable change, having credentials to attest that they had been to school, they are yet stuck on the stupidity of familiarity of their present, past failures and inabilities. They have transformed their insecurities into futuristic permanent inadequacies, as a result of failures and the inability to produce their own desired change.

People are always speaking of their own desired platforms of living, but their truest inability lies within the fact that they can never even hear themselves talking, at all. They have not all realized that the ability to change their own living atmospheres lie within themselves now haven been supplied the knowledge to amass a much greater platform of employment to produce income, and a more reasonable power to influence others. Most people are alike myself in that I don't have a problem or a situation that more money wouldn't solve in a hurry!

The struggle and the fight for centuries have been over the ability to obtain knowledge, and to become more productive people of society. People have shed blood and have spent many years locked away in prison for others to have the right just to study freely among the peers of their own equality, without prejudice.

As long as people were fighting for the right to go to school, those who were actually blessed with the opportunity to attend higher learning institutions, were more appreciative, and they even became advocates for learning. But now that it appears the struggle is just about over, more people appear to be apathetically uninterested, and completely turned off at the idea of working in their own chosen fields of study.

How smart is smart, and just exactly what constitutes educated intelligence, when an individual's behavior does not even reflect a propagated knowledgeable increase to distinguish between the derelicts and the Doctors, and the paupers and the Princes of the world?

Shouldn't the acquisition of knowledge that the people in our society are so influenced to expunge, be the difference in the behavioral quality of people, and not just the quality and quantity of their material possessions?

Many sermons preached in the churches suggest that; *"when you know better you will do better!"* It was my assumption that preachers were only making excuses for the behavior of many of the people, who were stubborn and rebellious to change; but, now I am sure that those messages were nothing more than inspirational cushions for certain people, who were slow to adhere to the teachings of the church.

My reference is not to the things that are purchased as result of being able to secure better jobs and to belong to sociable groups of community influences; I'm talking about the personal behavioral patterns of any educated individual, of whose behavior is no better than the average criminal, alcoholic, drug addict, rapist, sexual predator, and so on…………………………………

Knowing doesn't always solve the crisis of the perpetual inadequacies in the spirit and behavior of people. You would be totally shocked and blown away, at the knowledge that many people have acquired in their lives! People are neither stupid, nor illiterate as many may suppose that they are; but they are ignorant in that they omit to apply the acquired learning to their lives daily; or either they have been chocked full of the wrong kinds of knowledge, that has indeed driven them over the societal edges of living wrong.

Oh! And by the way the above mentioned vices are attached to many of the said, would be educated people of our society.

I have always been disturbed down in my spirit whenever it is reported in the media of educated child molesters and rapists, educated serial killers, extortionist, arsonist, bank robbers with Dr. degrees, and on and on and on...........................

Shouldn't it be said that these people knew better than to do the things that they did? Didn't their education set forth the precedence for a greater determination to live according to the laws of the land? Shouldn't they have been better equipped to resist the drive to attempt to get away with committing an evil act of violence against another?

Perhaps the emerging question is, "what does the behavior of people have to do with their levels of education?" Well I'm convinced that you're on the right track to where it is that I am interested in leading you to concentrate your thought process.

Knowing and doing are two totally different things! Learning should cause us to realize just how much we really don't know. The more knowledge that we are able to put into our minds, is a grave indicator that much knowledge was actually absent from our minds and our intellects!

112

Just because you know doesn't mean that you do what you actually know to do! It is the standard behavior of many people to do the opposite of what they have been instructed to do in any situation and on any platform. The smarter people become, they seem to intelligently realize just how much more there is to be learned.

There is absolutely positively nothing wrong with the acquisition of more knowledge, but we should grow as productive members of our society and as helpers to our fellowman. But, instead of growing, the average people of the higher levels of learning are only going..................?

They are going over the edges of living, mad and insane, to and fro throughout the world and the society dissatisfied and unable to adhere to the reality of living still on the earth with everyone else, they feel that they have become as gods; their eyes have become opened to speculate that many others do not have the knowledge they have, they believe anyway!

To engage in a conversation with certain educated people, you soon know for a fact that they have been to college institutions, because they go on and on and on and on, in the conversation trying to prove to you that they have more knowledge than the average person.

They are arrogantly on a journey to prove to as many people as possible that they have knowledge, as if knowledge is some sort of a new found treasure. It may in fact have been new to them, but somebody else already knew before them! Other people have definitely lived knowledgeably, before you!

Knowledge should not just make you go, it should cause you to grow! Whatever you do should be better in every since of the word as result of an enhanced knowledge to perform at a higher level as a better skilled worker and employee. Foolishly, people have been allowed to believe that knowledge makes them a better person, when the actual power of knowledge is only to make you a better educated individual.

Knowledge alone is not an escalator, but how you apply knowledge can often be an elevator under the guise of proper usage, among the people who apply the knowledge in the proper spirit and attitude. It's your attitude that determines you altitude!

Past the Exam; But Failed the Instruction

Many people test well in school, while taking exams to determine whether or not they had actually acquired the knowledge of the teacher, instructor, or the professor while sitting in their classroom sessions. We have all been

gravely misinformed to believe that just because people are passing the test that they have actually learned the information offered in the course of study.

Who's to blame for the failed acquisition of knowledge, when the knowledge has been set before those who should be interested in being knowledgeably equipped, as a result of the classroom instruction?

How does one explain having past a very demanding exam for the subject to which they have just spent weeks studying, only to reveal through their job performance, and/or their unparalleled behavior that is contrary to the knowledge that they were supposed to have acquired; that they hadn't been knowledgeably equipped after all?

It is one thing to study Subjects, and Topics of desired studies to increase the knowledgeable input in one's own intellect in the classrooms and institutions of learning, but it is altogether a totally different thing of respect whenever it comes to living applicable according to the lessons we have learned and have been taught.

However in all truthfullness, we don't live the subjects or the topics that are taught in the classroom. As it is, people come to the learning institutions from all of the many diverse walks of life and living to be enhanced as a result of the subjects and the topics of which they have studied.

What we have learned to live, relative to our family history, our neighborhoods and communities, and our churches and the laws of the government, through television media and all of the different types of reading materials, have trumped the ability to transform the psyche of the already established mental order/disorder in the average individual.

Even though people spend hours in the laboratories and the classrooms, the knowledge that they had already filed away in their own memory bank will have already made an indelible impression on their way of thinking to the point that they cannot change the cycle of their own thought process, or the ability to change the manner in which they move about their lives, daily.

It may also be fair to say that the number of the people of our society, who are educated, is much smaller in percentile to that of those who never entertain the thought of higher education, and even of those who went to school but dropped out before finishing the required hourly academic recommendation for completing the course of study.

With that all being said, the thought process of the lesser educated may often be less-enlightening and negatively resistant to the ideas of change, lacking the explanatory relevance that leads to the decisiveness for greater choices.

What is the true academic success rate in the volume of educated people, and how do we even go about to determine the rate of success, when those who have completed their course of studies are in the penal systems, locked away behind prison bars, in mental institutions, they're on probation for crimes committed, and even on death row awaiting execution? When we know better, do we really do better?

For we know that the law is spiritual: but I am carnal sold under sin. For that which I do I allow not: for what I would, that do I not; but what I hate that do I. If then I do that which I would not, I consent unto the law that it is good. Now then it is no more I that do it, but sin that dwelleth in me. For I know that in me (that is, in my flesh,) dwelleth no good thing: for to will is present with me; but how to perform that which is good I find not. For the good that I would I do not; but the evil which I would not, that I do. Now if I do that I would not, it is no more I that do it, but sin that dwelleth in me. I find then a law, that, when I would do good, evil is present with me. For I delight in the law of God after the inward man: But I see another law in my members, warring against the law of my mind, and bringing me into captivity to the law of sin which is in my members.

Romans 7: 14-23

Don't forget that my relevance is not to preschool aged children, or even to High School students; I'm talking about post High School graduates and adults who have gone on to higher learning....................................

Every wayward offending individual know their own mind, and the capabilities to commit acts that would never reflect the fact that they had indeed been to higher learning institutions, that should have enhanced their ability to be more productive to the society of which they live.

I am not here to try and convince anyone that we have over valued higher education; but perhaps we have misplaced education on the list of the priorities of living, and for sure we have misdiagnosed the status of being smarter, when it comes to corralling the behavior of the more knowledgeable individuals. What we learn doesn't determine who we are, but who we are does determine what we are able to learn!

It is not necessarily the responsibility of the teaching instructor to discern the actual character of the students, further determining whether or not they would be able to acquire the knowledge in the classroom. Rather, every student has knowledge of themselves, whereas they are the ones who know within themselves whether or not they are actually capable of acquiring the lessons being taught.

Even more so, the individuals know of whom they are before ever stepping into a classroom to participate in the offered topic of studies. Only, as a result of the post behavior after college graduation and sometimes while they are still in college do we perhaps gain a clear and more accurate idea of the reasons that most people have attended college.

What the instructor can never really know, are the reasons that certain students have chosen to attend their schools, even after probing to gain a since of knowledge of every individual student, all that can be gained from the explanations are the verbal or written statements given.

Many times, the very persons who were elected to be the most successful after graduation have been the very individuals to break the biggest, and the more grotesque stories in the

News Media. To the surprise of the learning institution, those people were actually no better off than those persons who stand on the street corners and peddle drugs, and elicit sex for money, having never attended college at all. Because these perpetrators worked so hard studying and researching knowledge, it was assumed that they would indeed be the difference makers in the society of which they were living.

They were supposed to encourage others around them to make the kinds of educated change that they, themselves should have made. Perhaps they never realized that they were being instructed in an effort to later instruct others, even if the people to whom they would be given to help would never attend any higher learning institutions? It's evident that they never psychologically processed the teaching or the instruction!   Some people even say; *"I took the course, but I never understood it; that professor was very hard!"*

Our society had been hurled into a tailspin several decades back, over drug-dealers, and criminals wearing the finer clothing, and driving the nicer high end, pricier automobiles, and living in the more luxurious homes, all because we as a nation and as a communal influx of people have

been dooped and deceived into believing that only the more educated people of the society who know more and are purported to being smarter as a result of learning, that only they would ever have those types of things for a possession.

Although our society has been working very hard, changing the laws, and watching the financial income records of every individual to determine whether a person could afford the things that they have for a possession; often citing that an individual had not even been through the training offered in the classrooms and institutions of higher learning, to be qualified to amass an income that would allow for such a comfortable level of living!

Society; still doesn't know how to prevent those that truly have a desire for living respectively on the top, who have not applied the higher learning institution's manner of acquiring their livelihood, from being able to do so, somehow the uneducated still acquire those things by hefty proportions!

Educated studies along doesn't ensure the possibilities of elevated living among the society's elite, even as having a lower level of scholastic achievements doesn't necessarily lessen the possibilities for climbing out of the lower levels of living on society's bottoms.

Why Do You Think It Is?

Educated Scientist; have always sought to encourage the individual usage of the mind over and above that of having faith in the unknown and the unseen. It has always been suggested that those who have enlightened their own minds through the elevated thought of education, would be somewhat better off to chart the pathways of their course of living, taking control of their own lives.

From as far back as history has been able to document, man seem to always down play the serious actuality of the written word of our Lord and savior Jesus Christ.

It was never the Lord's intention that we mature in our spirit and understanding to eventually leave the teachings of faith, and meditating on the word of God, to go about our own lives seeking to scientifically understand everything that there ever would be to understand through the thinking skills of our own minds. The bible does instruct us as believers to get an understanding; but, everythings is not available

for the mental exploration of our minds to the intent that we arrive at the ability to understanding; everything?

We are not given to live this human experience long enough to know everything there is to know. There is not one single person on the face of the planet who could ever say that they understand everything that there is to be understood. Human intelligence allows for us as individuals to become knowledgeable masters at certain chosen trades in life, but only one at a time!

Let's not take for granted that those who are indeed smart, that they have truly acquired a wealth of knowledge. In other words, they do know what they know; but they will never know everything. Only God knows everything! Inflated egos and pride have got many people thinking that they know more than they actually do know!

Although the abundance of knowledge is freely flowing through the earth, more swiftly than the wind blows through the trees, and the more fluid that the waves roll across the ocean's tides, just as we don't have containers to scoop up the ocean, neither do we have the capacities to expunge all of the knowledge in the world?

Here is a fact for your mind; it is our

responsibilities to gain knowledge for living here on the earth, but it is also our responsibilities to gain knowledge in the realm of the spirit as well. Knowing where we live does not counsel out the need to know how to live! How we play and recreate is not as important as how we worship and praise the Lord. What we have learned should never trump the origins of the information that we have acquired.

Many have become fools thinking that they have now become more knowledgeable than the teachers and instructors who were truly responsible for delivering the knowledge that they now have. You might want to consider the fact that you have only received the lessons! However, the teaching instructors have perhaps many years of applied experience of the same knowledge to which they have just delivered to you.

I have been told by many people who decided to put the bible down, giving up on the idea of ever being able to decipher the coded dialogue through their own literacy, they say that the bible is just too difficult to understand. They are very smart people, but, they have been forced to realize that their intelligence alone is no match for the written dialogue of the scripture.

Many people feel that the mysteries of the

bible should be left to the preachers at the church, and to the theologians at the biblical institutes of learning. Yet, by the same token, most people think that they themselves have got a comprehensive breakdown on all poetic dialogue, and any other literary works.

People sit under the cloud of what has been referred to as the "Spoken Word", feeling as if they are intellectually deep individuals, because they are able to breakdown riddles, interpret anomalies, and to understand the cynicisms buried beneath the rhythms of poetic reason and rhyms.

It is my own opinionated understanding that we should above all things, seek to understand why it is that we have chosen to identify with or at least to reasonably gamble our thinking process on certain issues of informational facts of learning, that alter our status of living.

Whether of the natural, or of the spiritual in nature, we would be so much better off if we only knew why it is that we have allowed those things to rest in our minds and on our hearts.

Why is it that we have taken in certain information which has the power to steer our thought process, taking hold of our emotions, to lasso and to spiritually dismember our physical ability to behave in the like manner of God? The light of the Lord can be clearly discerned, emanating from the inside of us, telling those who have witnessed our behavior, that we believe the written word of God, and it is available to them if they really desire to know.

I have found that even the most illiterate people have the audacity to try and examine the written word of God, as if to evaluate its authenticity; in hindsight of the fact that they have never examined anything else that have ever come their way!

What we often refer to as common since; would show everybody on the outside looking in, that if these persons would put a little time in to study and to closely examine the unread materials that have passed through their hands, their lives might be much more stable, and even financially secure.

Most people will go to their mail boxes to retrieve the mail that had been delivered that same day, but they take the mail and pitch it atop of the table, or in a designated place in their house, only never to pick it up to examine the contents in the envelopes.

Those persons are always the ones who find

themselves disgruntled as a result of having their utilities shutoff, and or their possessions repossessed; they have failed to open the bills in the mail, which told them of the due date for the payment of those same bills.

Alike the classroom, many are failing the tests of life simply because they refuse to study and to even read the required materials necessary for passing daily tests. In classrooms we learn to at least pick up the reading materials to literally examine them for the sake of class studies.

We know that if we do not at least pick it up, that we are never going to read the materials, which in turn will leave us indigent to past the test when given to examine our knowledgeable acquisition.

We Have Got To Know***

I can only imagine, what our surroundings would be like, if everyone understood why it is that they do accept all of the things that they mentally comprehend in their own thought process, and what it actually means to their own livelihood as a productive individual.

Do you know the meaning behind the

127

information to which you have chosen to indulge yourself, or have you only accepted it because it has been written and read, or because it has been spoken and heard of you?

People in a classroom get it when the professor says to them, to go home and read 3-6 chapters of the textbook for the course. They know that if they are going to keep up with the course that they themselves are going to have to comply with the requirements for the class. However, whenever the same people of the churches are told to go home and to read 3-6 chapters of the bible, they have a problem, and can't seem to get with the required request of the leadership of the church.

Here's Why: The bible being the word of God; is firstly a spiritual book, whereas the spirit of God embodies, engulfs and encircles the wording on every page. Which also means that whenever you get the word of God on the inside of your spirit, through the acceptance of the word in your mind, you are also going to get the spirit God on the inside of your belly, which in turn will poignantly alter your behavior.

The spirit of God is powerful; therefore the powerful spirit of God now down on the inside of your belly is going to take the control, and to

arrest every other spirit on the inside of you, to produce change.

When our behavior begins to change right before our very eyes, having the word of God as the driving enforcer down on the inside of our belly, we have the very necessary explanation to answer for the purported behavior that is now being projected.

We need the word of God to answer and to speak up for us in times of inquisitions, when others will be compelled to ask a reason of the hope that is within us, and why it is that we have chosen to disconnect from the ways of the world and from the hidden behavior of sin.

It is not at all acceptable to lack explanation of the God on the inside of you. The days of just doing church stuff, and identifying with religious affiliations as the total extent of the knowledge that we have relative to God, are swiftly closing out! God always intended for us to know why, what, how, when, where, and definitely who as it relates to knowing God and our relationship with Him. So; just how smart are you really, when you don't know?

Scene 7

The Library[*]

Then said I, Lo, I come (in the volume of the book it is written of me,) to do thy will, O God, HEBREWS 10:7

Latin —bibliotheca—Library

Greek —bibliotheke—Library

La-Biblios —The Books---Archives

The Place of Safe Keeping*

Although the word library is not used in the actual writing of the bible, the word bible is actually originated from the word which means library. The compilation of canonized writings which make up the 66 books of the bible are the original archive collections of penned accounts that lend the knowledgeable record of God's creative works and the relationship with man in the earth.

We recognize the library as a place for storing the finished literary works of multiple authors on every subject possible for acquiring knowledgeable enlightenment. I have always regarded the library as a place of silent solitude in surrender where we escape to listen to self and our reasonable selection of reading, or to study materials for the purpose of building and enhancing the mental physique. (If you will allow me)

Our teaching from even our early childhood learning experiences urge us to respect the library as being a place to soar in motionless travel through the pages of documented scripts to further realize the vast world. Many people may never board a plane to visit a foreign land that have boarded the pages of a book, figuratively speaking, in the library to view in detail, the land

and countries in which they were indeed curious.

Every institution has its own archive of safe keeping where people visit to be enlightened of the institution and the given instruction offered in its classroom sessions. Even though labs are a very important part of institutional instruction, the library holds the definitive relevance to all of the researchable findings, acquired in a laboratory.

Whatever we find is not as important as knowing what we have actually found. Further knowledge of our findings tells us what to do with what we have found and how to properly manage and to maintain the treasure of our findings. Such knowledge is often housed in the library on the shelf, alphabetized for narrowing our search in a timely manner.

Adam and Eve tripped the lever that would never be shut off. They opened up a can! The knowledge that flows to us is both good and evil judging the content and the source from which it flows to us. Let me establish that there is some knowledge that is bad, although it is believed that knowledge is always good, it has likewise been further determined that what we choose to do with knowledge eventually qualifies the knowledge as bad.

Knowledge has never ceased to flow through all of the created realms of mankind. The tree has been pumping out knowledge ever since the day that Adam and Eve ate of the tree. Being that Adam was so much more like God than we of these latter generations of the earth, I am not sure that I could truthfully say that we are actually smarter now than they were there in the garden, and be able to qualify the statement with undeniable facts.

It is dangerous to lack mental strength when living in the kingdom of God, as there will always be those who strongly oppose the reality and the deity of God, who will consistently launch an offensive attack against individuals in the body of Christ. You've got to be strong!

No matter how good a person you may in fact be, there is some knowledge that will eventually cause you to become corrupt should you apply it to your life.

Be not deceived, evil communication corrupt good manners.   I CORINTHIANS **15:33**

Relative To The Tree*

Isn't it amazing that the library is referred to as a branch? Remember the release of knowledge into the earth's realm started with a tree that had been loaded with knowledgeable flavornoids in each succulent bite of the delicious fruit of the tree. As far as we know, only a few bites of the tree released enough knowledge to last throughout all the reign of humanity over the entire earth.

Most public libraries are referred to as Branch Libraries, which are sub-divisions to the Central library often located in the heart of the center section of the city. The main library of the city is similar to the tree trunk which is the stabalized base to all of its extended branches. No matter how far the branches are extended from the centralized position of the trunk, they gracefully reach out as a living part of the tree.

The branches of the tree, often referred to as the limbs, are what offers the shading effect from the intensity of the heat of the sunlight on hot summer days. God in His infinite wisdom, He knows that too much open exposure to the sunlight could possible be damaging to the earth's surface and to the inhabitants of the land as well. Therefore branches were necessary to find a place to shelter from the intensity of the heat rays.

We often focus on the foliage of the trees as only being the identifying beauty of the tree; whereas, the individually unique design of the leaves on the branches of the different trees have the ability to silently speak the names of the trees. Trees appear to have similar traits in the bark which can make it difficult to identify during the winter months when the leaves are fallen to the ground.

There is so much more to the tree than what

we may be able to see. The leaves and the tender branches of the trees provide food source for many of the animals in the wild. Beavers, chew down trees with their powerful teeth to build an habitat for them in the river.

When Adam and Eve realized that they had sinned and crossed the uncrossable line, they turned to the tree and borrowed it's leaves to cover themselves, shielding themselves from their nakedness. Here's Why: Their nakedness was to the likes of a newly born infant; they were brand new to the reality of their humanness.

At birth; we're naked without covering in many forms, other than our skin and hair. As an infant we lacked everything necessary to suffice a lifestyle conducive to living among other people, incapable of decisive reasoning. Even the under-development of our brains could not allow us to take advantage of the wealth of knowledge looming about our heads in our present atmospheres.

As Adam and Eve were driven away from the tree, Adam was commanded to "till the earth." In other words, man would have to dig for the knowledge of God and for the knowledge of mankind from now on!

Man would also be in the state of remembering where they had indeed come from, dreading the fact that one day we are destined to return to the dust of the same earth that we are now commanded to till. Tilling the earth put man in a state of continuously looking downward, putting pressure on us as mankind to lookup to God, in effort to find the rekindling of the former lost relationship between God and man.

God; being so vast, He knows that the knowledge of Himself would have to be broken into measures of knowledgeable inputs for the sake of not allowing man to choke on the mega-truth of the reality of His existence, being too much to swallow at once, and far too much to be obtained in one learning session.

So, even as the trees have many branches to shade the earth, the library has many ampli-fied extended branches all over the earth since the garden experience to shade the vast world of knowledge. The tree lived; therefore sprouting its branches to all regions of the world.

While eating from the tree produced a death sentence for all mankind, death was never pro-nounced over the tree.

What most men have not realized, is that the libraries are at best extended branches of the original tree in the midst of the garden of Eden, established to house the finished creative works of authors.

Equally fascinated and gullible of knowl-edge on any level; if it is available to be received, people want it no matter what! No matter where it comes from, or what it is designed to do, when presented as a possible learning option, people don't dare miss the opportunity to give their un-divided attention to the presentation.

The Place of Remembering*

The library is where we mindfully reconnect by the way of written documents prepared for the purpose of telling past occurrences, but true accounts of God's interaction with man. If it were not for the shelved accounts from the past, many people would be permanently lost and deterred to believe on the past record of the power of God.

As we preach and teach about what God has done, from Genesis to Revelation; the actual accounts of the hand of God moving, lends to the memorial recall that will enable others to grasp the reality of a God who is involved with the affairs of the people of the earth.

I have said in prior writings; that many people are determined to embrace the God that was, rather than to acknowledge the God that is!

It is understandable that the written accounts of God's past works are accounts that concluded there per the expiratation of each writer. The writer might have stopped there, but God continued to move forward progressing throughout the faithful community of believers.

God is infinite in His never beginning and never ending reign of eternal existence. We as human beings are finite: we begin from the date of our birth, to the actual date of our death. 1907-2007?

We have a starting point and a stopping point, therefore our ability to know is as limited as our ability to swim the entire ocean. What's more amazing is that even a gigantic Ocean-Liner designed to cruise the ocean for many miles, can only cover so much of the ocean over any period of time. All is never an option!

It's time that *we* view knowledge in light of many oceans in its vastness. The actual flow of knowledge is too swift for the brain waves of most individuals. Knowledge swirls like that of a whirlpool in swift running currents in a roaring rapid river. Even well trained swimmers can drown when caught in its currents.

Many people can blow their own minds out of shape attempting to handle too much knowledge, not having a refined purpose for the knowledge in the first place. Knowledge will inflate the ego of an individual without them even knowing that they are entered into egotistical arrogance. The apparent fact that other people have not acquired the same level of knowledge that you have, can be imminent danger for you!

Shh! Quite Please!*

Many people don't really care that they do you a disservice when talking all of the time in your ears, but you ought to care about the disservice that you do to yourself listening to them!

Back in kindergarten; we were taught to put our index finger to our mouths, to ask our classmates to stop talking while we were in the library. Some of them got the message, while others ignored the request. We were taught the importance of being quiet in the library. But, what they could not teach us, was the purpose for being quiet in the first place, being that we were too immature to grasp the teaching,

I matured to realize that we would be entering the library to study for the rest of our educated lives, to research the stored data on the shelves from every topic possible. The key word here is "Study!"

Study-the effort to learn by reading or thinking: a careful examination; investigation: earnest effort; deep thought; usually with respect for the ability to memorize. (World Book Dictionary)

In my own opinion; mental incompetence is not necessarily always the result of an illness of the mind; it is often gravely, the intentional mental distractions from others who have the power of influence over that individual. It's not possible to concentrate when someone else is talking! Reasonable decisions must be well thought out rations of the mind.

Some people simply, sinfully do not wish for you to research the stored archive of God in the memorial library recall among the people that have experienced God! It's about time that you realized people are talking against the move and the knowledge of God only for the purpose of blocking your ability to hear Him when He speaks to your heart.

They're determined that you be so confused that you wont be able to clearly discern God's unmistakable voice when hear Him, and you will! You will find yourself thinking that it's the devil or something that you might have eaten just prior to hearing Him speak to you.

Only the voices of other people can actually have this effect on an individual. It has been reported many times over that a drunkard, or even a junkie stoned out of their mind heard the voice of God and they immediately became sober, as if they had never taken a drink or used any drug.

To use drugs and to drink alcohol, are all things that you will do to yourself; but to be influenced to the point that you have been blocked from hearing the voice of God speaking to your heart, is what other people will do to you!

> *And that ye study to be quiet, and to do your own business, and to work with your own hands, as we commanded you;*
>
> I THESSALONIANS 4:11
>
> *Study to shew thyself approved unto God, a workman that needeth not to be ashamed, rightly dividing the word of truth.*
>
> II TIMOTHY 2:15

A very common belief in the churches nowadays, is that we need to go back and study what we've been taught, all over again? But, consider the fact that we had already studied and had been taught, having cluttered, chaotic, confused, and extremely unsettled minds?

It's like trying to plant a tree in the midst of an earth-quake! The ground itself is too shaky for anyone to dig a hole into the earth, to place the tree into the ground.

The ground cannot be shaking or unstable, as everything and everyone will likely be unstable for any purpose. How much knowledge can be acquired when our minds have been shaken and stirred causing us to question every minute detail of every word that comes into our minds, before ever settling to properly examine as acceptable or not?

Don't be fooled into believing that you are intelligent to question receiving knowledge as it relates to God; otherwise being taught to be as opened minded as possible to any other knowledge that comes from secular studies and science. Thinking yourselves to be wise, which is characteristical of God; you will actually become knowledgeable fools.

It is not necessary to continue to study as if we have never learned anything. We may miss certain details while studing various topics of discussion, but most of us are prone to acquire a great deal more than we would ever miss. We are studious enough to take in the knowledge, only the storage places of the mind may have invariable instabilities, capable of shutting out the acquired input.

We need very desperately to examine our minds that are used to study and to acquire knowledge in every form. The inaccurate filters of the mind are often alternatively defiled and damaged, as a result of the outright determination to sin. We convince ourselves that we are yet righteous, even when we've choosen sin above the righteous of Christ.

Instead of ignoring the dreadful times of which we are living, we need to take hold of ourselves vigorously challenging what we're thinking throughout the run of the day. Without the proper knowledge from the word of God to direct us and to prevent us from being infiltrated with corrupt knowledge we are hopelessly in danger of losing our way through life, and the loss of our soul in eternity.

Jesus confronted the Jews because they thought they knew everything about God already, though they were very religious, they never knew God by HIs spirit. They thought they'd add pressure to the pressure cooker and cause Him to defy the mercy of His own grace. They wanted to see Jesus perofrm in certain circumstances.

Jesus knew what they were thinking before they could act upon their thoughts. Before they could move, Jesus had already made a countermove leaving them baffled and bewildered. They were too busy thinking about all of the wrong things, all of the time. The wrong thinking will absolutely never lead to making the right decisions.

> *Search the scriptures; for in them ye think ye have eternal life: and they are they which testify of me. Do not think that I will accuse you to the Father: there is one that accuseth you, even Moses, in whom ye trust. For had ye believed Moses, ye would have believed me: for he wrote of me. But if ye believed not his writings, how shall ye believe my words?* ST. JOHN **5:39; 45-47**
> *Then said I, Lo, I come (in the volume of the book it is written of me,) to do thy will, O God.* HEBREWS **10:7**

People think that they already know, until they open the pages of a book to find that they did not even have the slightest possible clue; the knowledge that they had was indeed all wrong. Questions are answered wrong because we failed to study the true answers to the equations. People get the wrong information and take off with the knowledge as reliable, only to suffer great defeat, and loss as result of the misinformation.

Jesus tells the Jews to search the scripture; He gives them the recipe to be sure within themselves that they know who Jesus really is. The

Jewish scholars spent some time in the library, but they failed to know that the very beginning of knowledge was literally standing in their presence, to impart a greater knowledge of Himself to them.

Jesus knew the Jews were mere seekers of carnal knowledge, being readers of the scrolls of those days. Had they believed what Moses had written of Him, they wouldn't have problems receiving Him. The scrolls and the Torah were read in the synagogue. The scrolls were consistent of scriptures from the Old Testament, and perhaps a few other writings that might not have been canonized in the 66 books.

The Jews read in the writings of Moses, and were very familiar with biblical prophecies of the coming Messiah; yet still they don't believe that the Holy bible is actually for us today. The Jews have problems with spiritual revelatory insight and the manifested word of God, which was indeed standing in their presence. The Jewish national community have not all completely come forward to embrace Jesus Christ as the promised Messiah. (messenger from God)

People are stuck on history lessons in all learning institutions, as long as the lessons are referenced with no present day implicative connotations. Even in the church people believe that whatever happened yesterday, relative to biblical references and early church historical beginnings, was only for yesterday, and that today warrants brand new experiences, even if no lessons have been learned from the experiences of yesterday.

Erroniously; people are now feeling as if we need to progress beyond the message of the gospel of Jesus Christ; and the teachings of holy and righteous living.

It is obvious that people have begun reading the wrong books. Just as there is a historical account of God and His righteous, there is also the history of sinfully selfish ungodly living. The development of man has taken on a more godless form in spirit. People have developed a more sinister appetite for iniquitous living.

A few decades ago, more people went to church, and had a healthier respect for God, and cared for the wellbeing of their fellowman. Remember; that this was the one nation under God; with liberty and justice for all! We used to believe that there is only one God who is the Father and the creator of all mankind; now we have the infiltrated idealism of polytheistic god's introduced by way of the social media, and other written data.

Here Is What I Mean**

A building itself, is not what makes for the qualifications of a library! Where the building is actually located in the city, or the square footage of the room and the shelves on the walls, also do not make the building a library. I have many books on the shelf and many small stacks in my home, but that doesn't qualify my house to dubbed a library.

However, the sanctified spiritual data that is stored in my mind, soul, and spirit does qualify as being a library. I have as much information stored there; as the information stored in all of the books in my house.

Book shelves in large rooms in big buildings is not what qualifies the building as a library. Book stores are often set up in a very similar manner as the library, but the actual purpose of the businesses divides the definitive structure of the buildings. Book depositories and storage facilities also house large quantities of books, but the purpose for housing the books is not for the availability of researching stored data.

Some libraries have more shelves, thus they have more books; doesn't make it to be more of a library than the library that has a lesser quantity of books and shelves. Some compete to see who has the most knowledge of the bible, and the number of college degrees. Some even compare the archive of lifetime experiences that lend to the broader scope of reasoning, for which we apply the wisdom of God. There will always be someone who will have acquired more than someone else.

It's not always about what you know as much as it is about what you do as a result of what you know! We acquire knowledge that suggest certain behavioral patterns necessary to acquire vocational skills and trades. Likewise we may also collide with knowledge that suggest a reasonable right to do the very opposite of the knowledge acquired.

Naturally speaking, the library has limited hours of access, whereas we are not always freely permitted to partake of the fruitful preparations in the written dialogue on the branches of the library tree at our own discretion.

In retrospect; the atmosphere of which we live everyday of our lives, is a library archive of the handiwork of God, open unto us 24 hours a day, 7 days a week. We stand in this library but we often fail to partake of the vast knowledge of our surrounding world, to enhance our integrity and the knowledge of God.

We have never read in the scriptures that Adam and Eve had identity crises or if they ever ask the God of all creation, "who are we?" They're the ones responsible for this extreme exposure to knowledge being availably unleashed on humanity in the first place; they knew about knowing before we ever knew about learning!

Being the fore-parents of humanity; there are some things that are naturally inherent to us that we should not have found ourselves still asking the Lord to reveal to us. But, because we have forsaken the heritage of our true beginning, we have also been denied the knowledge of our true

identity.

Although God drove them out of the garden of Eden; God did not kill them and recreate mankind all over again. They were the same as they were in the garden even before they ate from the tree, only they were knowledgeable people who now know more than just God; of which was the initial excellent state of mankind, knowing the personal excellence of God; alone.

People spend months and even years searching their bloodline history, and their family archive, trying to gain a knowledgeable scope of family to define who they are. We have been led to believe that if we search the family tree, we would find the true linage of our existence.

Many people have tried searching the medical record of births back to several generations, only to discover that there have been missing and sometimes falsified documents that hinder the discovery of the search. When desiring to lean on such paper trails, we stand to risk the loss of the necessary data that would enable us to know who we are and who we have always been!

Science has psyched humanity to the point that people no longer believe that they can turn to God for the purpose of finding out who they are. Of course science has also over stepped its boundaries with the intent to define the reality of God; sometimes through scientific disproof. People continue to search; while never finding the concrete reasoning to excuse their behavior for acting out their choices of living in ways that are contrary to the word and the will of God!

For the invisible things of him from the creation of the world are clearly seen, being understood by the things that are made, even his eternal power and Godhead; so that they are without excuse: ROMANS **1:20**

The laws of the land don't change just because they are broken and transgressed; neither does the laws of God change nor warrant being changed simply because people neither choose or desire to obey the laws of God! Therefore people may always continue to search the laws of God, but they will never ever find any excuse in the laws of God that will allow them to continue to behave themselves in the manner that is offensive to the word of God.

We understand the punishment for offensive behavior to the laws of the land, whenever a judge will impose the penalty fit for a crime committed. It seems to taken it with a grain of salt! People are willing to admit that what they did was indeed wrong as far as the law is concerned, though they might have felt that they had a validated reason to do whatever they did.

On the other hand, I have seen some people go to their graves who never admitted to God that they were wrong for living their lifestyles in ways that never brought glory to the name of the Lord,

never repented or sought the Lord for forgiveness. Many think that they can take going to hell just as they feel that they are tough enough to take a prison sentence, they are mean enough to face challenges behind prison bars.

The two scenarios are the ultimate differences between life in the natural and life in the spiritual realm. We need to search the library archive of God's record, to know what things in our lives need to be cleaned up and repaired. God is available to help us through the power of the shed blood of Jesus Christ. Jesus Christ is the only way, that God can help us; no matter what you might have been led to believe!

Many people are missing the knowledge of God's love for us, and our need to respond to God accordingly. I have not met a sinner who has never heard that God is Love. They take the love of God for granted, and they continue to believe that God is not concerned with the manner in which they conduct themselves.

Most sinners, are very knowledgeable in many areas of studies in the secular scholastic arenas. They purposefully skip the knowledge of God thinking that they will have an excuse for escaping the judgment of hell, possibly citing the fact that they never knew! Ignorance is no excuse of the law!

Come unto me all ye that labour and are heavy laden, and I will give you rest. Take my yoke upon you, and learn of me; for I am meek and lowly of heart: and ye shall find rest unto your souls. For my yoke is easy and my burden is light.

ST. MATTHEW **11:28-30**

There is nothing about God that He won't reveal to you if you ask and seek Him with all of your heart. Many people will say that; "I am already saved; I already have God, through Jesus Christ in my life!"

Just because you have possession of a book, it doesn't mean that you have read the book. Actually; what good is it to have the book if you never read it, although you may have the intention to read it. Many will look at the book, but they will never look in the book.

Likewise, tons of people are owners of several bibles, with many translations and languages, but they rarely have the knowledge of a few scriptures. The bible was never intended for being the center piece on the living room table, or just another decorative piece on the mantle of the fireplace.

It is not until the pages of the bible have been cracked open that the realization comes into focus that the bible is the living word of God. That's right; the bible is alive, and it is the end of your search if you would take the time to look on the inside of the covers.

For I know the thoughts that I think toward you, thoughts of peace, and not of evil, to give you an expected end. Then shall ye call upon me, and find me, when ye shall search for me with all your heart. And ye shall seek me, and find me, when ye shall search for me with all your heart. And I will be found of you, saith the Lord: and I will turn away your captivity, and I will gather you from all of the nations, and from all the places whither I have driven you. Saith the Lord; and I will bring you again into the place whence I caused you to be carried away captive.

JEREMIAH **29:11-14**

Let me encourage you not to just look for a reason of authority to equalize your behavioral status, only to gauge the standard of your character against someone that's worse off than you!

Refine your search and start looking for God. Time is your gift; don't allow the sand to run out of the hourglass before you have found what you've been looking for. Also change the wisdom of your search and take your exploration to the library. Get out of the box that limit's the possibilities of your search, and look in the spread of God's domain of this Cosmo centric reality.

The hour of opportunity has now approached you, it's up to you to take advantage of the presentation of the open invitation to bask in the knowledge of the one and the only true and living God. He's been waiting for you to come, even in the middle of your struggles and your confusion, the Lord want's you to come to Him with the baggage in exchange for His blessings.

In this life we have to pay for what we get, but in God; we get what He has already paid for! In our world we have to see in order to believe, but in God; we believe God in faith in order to see the manifestation of our desires!

Earlier in this chapter I talked about mankind having to dig for the knowledge of God from now on; but, since Jesus came to the earth to save us and to redeem us back to God; all it takes is a sincere surrender from us, and God will reveal Himself to us. As we mature and our faith in God grow, the more of God we will begin to know.

Study to know everything about God that enables you to be more like Him. Allow your atmosphere to be transformed into a Heavenly atmosphere, that is conducive for angelic visitation and for the presence of the glory of God.

In the library you will soon discover that God won't mind if you have a Heaven experience right here, right now while you walk in the natural realm of your being.

In the historical recall in God's library, there are many patriarchs who have the knowledge that we might have been desiring. Won't it be wonderful to talk to those who have gone on before us, even before we were born, and even before our parents and grandparents were thought of, to

hear them talk about the experiences that they had with God only to realize that their stories mirror the exact details of our stories, being that God is the same; he never changes.

At the tomb of Jesus; the angels standing there in white raiment ask the question; "why seek ye the living among the dead?"

Don't be fooled into thinking that you are looking for an historical savior who was, being the only reason that you might find a record of Him in the Library! The angels also said to Mary Magdalene; "He is risen just as He said!" Jesus didn't sneak back to the grave after all was said and done to lay back down in the grave, He got up to stay up forever! Jesus is alive and well forever more!

John the revelator was on the isle of Patmos, in exile for preaching and teaching in the name of Jesus, for which he and the disciples had been forbidden to teach and to preach in that name. While on the island alone all by himself, the spirit of the Lord caught him up and took him to the library before the throne of God in Heaven.

John heard the voice of the son of God saying to him; "I am He that was dead; but now I am alive forever more!" "I am He which was, and is, and is to come!"

The conquering Christ revealed himself to John the Apostle! There must have been something special about the John's search that caused God to discover Himself to the man of God!

It really doesn't matter what your calling is, you won't see God unless you have a desire to see Him in the fullness of His power, and in the brightness of His glory. Those of us who look for Jesus and find Him now, won't be surprised and devastated to see Him when He cracks the sky, at His return, to receive His own out of the earth.

The door is open, step forward and enter in, turn right, go straight and continue in that direction! There you will find Jesus!

Then said I, Lo, I come (in the volume of the book it is written of me,) to do thy will , O God,   HEBREWS **10:7**
Who hath believed our report? And to whom is the arm of the Lord revealed?
ISAIAH **53:1**

He's in the Library!

Epilogue

Three Parts

A. Once: More Than Necessary

B. The Scheme of Satan and Sin

C. The Lasting Bite Marks

Once Bitten Forever

And when the woman saw that the tree was good for food, and that it was pleasant to the eyes, and a tree to be desired to make one wise, she took of the fruit thereof, and did eat, and gave also to her husband with her; and he did eat.

Genesis 3:6

Once: More Than Necessary***

This liturgical comprehensive dialogue of the tree of Knowledge of Good and Evil; has been a gifted delight to permissively approach such a highly debated topic as of my own spiritual assignment, to give enhanced revelatory insight to the body of Christ at large.

Understand me; it is far beyond the time of finding out exactly where the knowledge ability of the many smart people of the Universe originated, and what's really behind it from a very spiritual standpoint.

Most people often equate their intelligence with their family's history, even though those who were from the past generations just ahead of the present, many of them were often scholastically challenged, whereas they hardly had any schooling. They were not awarded the same advantage to advance into education and studies alike the present generations.

We really can't qualify any adjustable reasoning's, suggesting whether or not this generation's ability to deeply explore the diverse realms of knowledge was actually a blessing or a curse?

Scholars from the past that have been noted and documented as having been extremely smart, intelligent and even brilliant; but the questions often arrive as to how, and even where the knowledge acquired was actually made available to them. Who started them to thinking the way that they were eventually found to think?

Since becoming the innovative, sophisticated collaboration of thought provoking society which has produced the more civilized era of living and learning; with the respect of now, it has become an even greater necessity to embrace the past thinkers and scholars, as if to swing wide open the back doors to history revealing those countless unheard of teachers, and instructors.

Their past contributions to the shelves of knowledge, that are collectively responsible for the present products of intelligence which framed the current advanced technological depth of our own human dominance of the earth must be recognized.

Many people are standing by the ways of life with their chests pumped high towards the sky, with pointed noses of pride, and nasty dispositions, disgustingly seeing themselves as actually being greater than other human beings! But, often without the true understanding that there are hidden explosions right in the midst of the knowledge to which they are so proud. All that they have come to know over a process of time, can, and it will at times, blow up right back in their own faces!

Learning can often be held comparative to the delight of enjoying a favorite desert; once you dip into the container, it becomes very easy to return to the delight to repeat partaking of the very delicious contents in the container.

Once a knife has slit a cake, it doesn't get dulled for haven done so; as a result, we know that we are at the advantage to return to the mound of the cake to slice it again, whether it is good and healthy for us or not, we know that it's good to us!

Well so it is, with learning that is indeed being poured into us, whereas we have discovered that we are truly being taught by the way of the true excellence of a teaching instructor, we are often driven to return to learning atmospheres, even before daily applying the information to our lives that we have already acquired.

We often watch the television game shows like Jeopardy, Wheel of Fortune, and Pyramid just to name a few; while we marvel over the contestants who blurt out knowledge of things that we have never heard of our entire lives, thinking that they must be so much smarter than the average person on the planet.

They know too much stuff that will never even be applicable to their daily living, being that often a vast portion of the knowledge that they have acquired, is actually historical, therefore obsolete to our present lifestyles.

Once the show's over, the knowledge acquired is actually good for nothing else but another contest show of the same like caliber. There is nothing wrong with knowing a lot of things, however we ought to qualify the things that we allow to float around in our heads. The things that we know ought to benefit our daily lives, and our spiritual welfare. To what benefit is it to know a lot of things for nothing?

Foolishly, many knowledgeable people have allowed their own minds to box up the written word of God to be nothing more than a history book. They're convinced that we don't need the bible now.

As of recent, I have come into contact with many people who have have become extremely way too analytical! Their heads are so big and fat with knowledge, that it's always in the way of their ability to just do stuff, and just plain ole'

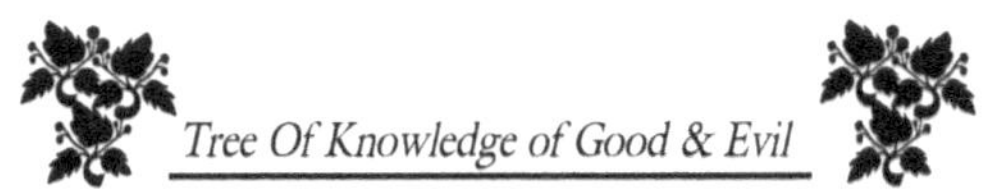

living, because everything has to make since and agree with their ability to process data. Their super-smart thinking is not necessary for the meager tasks set before them on a daily basis.

Everything has to scientifically jog with their understanding; this piece has to fit that piece, or either some sort of an equation has to create a smart solution; they're too smart for their own good!

People tell me that they cannot believe in God because it just did not make since to them that a savior would die on a cross, be buried in a grave, and then just get up out of the grave after three days.

When at best you are only analytical and not at all faithful, you will never be able to receive the finished work of the cross of Calvary, it takes faith and trust in the Lord to believe it, and then you can receive it.

Just exactly how much knowledge can one person apply to their lives whereas it becomes apparent to everyone who come into contact with them, that they are so wonderfully indulged with knowledge; and why?

Everyone has been given to the same exact levels of studying and knowledge, not everyone that we come into contact with are going to be

interested with how smart another individual just might be. To be perfectly honest; nobody even likes a know it all!

Most overly educated people are looked upon as being weird and abnormal to society, and are often referred to as being a "smart-alik." Many people who have common levels of understanding will often avoid contact with over indulgers.

It can be rather difficult to conversationally dialogue with those people because their minds are often moving too rapidly on another plain or sphere, whereas even their own personal points of interest are not at all the same as that of the more common individual.

For sure, every man ought to be so much smarter since Adam made the sinful error of touching and eating of the tree in the midst of the garden; but truthfully, it's not been the case that men have learned from the mistakes of another. As men of these later generations, we are still digesting that same bite; we have to see for ourselves!

In other words we are still smitten as a result of that very same devastating lie back in the garden, whereas we are still touching and eating those things that were forbidden by God.

I'm not really sure that Adam had the ability

to think about the generations afar off, and the forever rippling effect that his disobedience would have on the future generations of the entire population of the earth for the many years to come, before once biting the forbidden fruit.

Perhaps he never took himself as seriously as God did in the first place; in that after all he was just a man; a human being?

Remember the serpent told them that would be like gods, in that they would know things that they had never known; their eyes would become opened.....................................

It is forever important that we as the people of the Lord silence the voice of Satan speaking to our minds and spirits, and even the spirit of our minds; through prayer.

Satan is forever determining to set you up for the greatest failure of your life, if you allow him to do so.

People Satan is still at work blowing the minds of men and women alike, beguiling, and causing them to think and to believe that having knowledge and being smart is all that it takes to be like God!

People are running to and fro, seeking more and more knowledge everywhere they can get it; while they are gravely overlooking the bible!

Now being wordsmiths and scholars, we have the ability to objectively examine the stories of the bible to further determine the depth and the purported authenticity of the written matters in the 66 books of the bible since we are able to stand on the outside of the book of the bible and examine every word, as result of our word knowledge, dictionaries, and libraries.

The Scheme of Satan and Sin***

The exact point and time of the occurrences in the garden, took place at a time in the history of mankind that the challenges of such crimes as identity theft and undermining schemes were not yet heard of. Satan stole our identity from us and have been successful convincing us of just who we are not! We as people yet struggle to be realigned with who we are in the Lord, here in the earth!

We dread the sinful fallout of the disobedience back in the garden, yet we lean on that same fall as a crutch to continue in the ways of sin and shame, citing that after all we are only human beings who have proven over and over again that we could not obey God?

We blame Adam and Eve, for the present status of humanity, while we have overlooked the real predicament tucked away and hidden underneath the dilemma! Satan was up to something much bigger and so much more devastating than that which has been exposed and made knowledge to mankind. We squirm, complain and bicker over the pains of suffering as a result of sin and iniquity, thinking to ourselves just how terrible a thing sin is, actually?

Most people that even acknowledge that sin is indeed a TERRIBLE THING, they often find themselves asking the questions; why is it so bad, that God would never allow it into the presence of His glory and into Heaven? Of course the motives for the questions are merely self motivated, in that people would love to be able to sin at all points never being held accountable for their actions of choice.

People blame God for the abundant availability of sin's choices at such high volumes and magnitudes. They say; *"why, would the Lord put these things here if He did not want me to indulge in them?"* The focus is all wrong; we often refuse to take the responsibility for the actions that are indeed offensive to the word of God, and counterproductive to the movement of the spirit of the Lord in the earth.

We know that we have done wrong; we just want someone else to pay the penalty for the actions that we have committed! *"I did wrong and somebody is going to pay for it; just not me! Please........."*

People are at the churches seeking the Lord for ways to get beyond doing the types of things that have had them crying their eyes out over the guilt and the shame for committing those sins and

dodging other spiritual people of the churches, too embarrassed to face them knowing that they have not been living up to par, relative to the moral standards of living according to the bible. And of course I will not overlook the inner-church crowd who are blatant sinners, living out loud with no shame it appears; they project that if others can do it then so can they!

Then of course many; and at times even most people go on the defensive when caught in the wrong possibly on the brink of total exposure, they fight for the right to be just as sinful as the next person, being a human being, not needing to have their hidden deeds exposed.

Sin has got such a nasty sting attached to it that even those who have reported that they do not believe that sin is wrong, not even they themselves appreciate being found in the wrong.

Even some who had been theoretical devil worshippers, they really didn't totally admit to being as sinful as they really are, they tried to excuse themselves as only haven been experimental to the idea of Satanism!

Defensive people will also make the attempt to turn the spotlight on to the other culprit in the sinful equation. Perhaps, let's say that an official of the church gets caught with their hand

169

in the teal, in an effort to avoid going down all by themselves, they begin to pull the covers off of all of the others involved in the plot, even if their only part in the equation was as simple as being knowledgeable of the persons wrong doings, but they covered them up!

Alike criminals caught foul in a criminal plot, charged with the crime and facing jail time in the penitentiary, they turn states evidence against another to avoid the extremity of their own penalty or even to avoid being penalized at all.

Adam when in the presence of God after having disobeyed the commandment of God, he begin telling God about the woman that God had given to him, as if to suggest that it wasn't his fault. People still do this today, but they are lacking the true knowledge that would better serve the understandable reasoning for their own sinful actions.

There is a whole lot more of Satan in your sins than you might have realized! Most of us would not really want to acknowledge the fact that sin is and that it has been attached to us for any extended period of time simply because we don't desire for other people to believe that we have had any true personal dealings whereas

Satan had been in charge of our lives, but sin reveals just who is in charge of your life.

Every time that we put our hands to any type of sin, we have also put our hands out to Satan; Satan is definitely in the midst of sin, and iniquity and every transgression of the law of God. Every time that you even say sin, you have spoken the name of Satan, as sin is Satan's own creation even though it was God who informed Satan, the fallen angels, and every other human being that would participate in the evil plot of Satan, to call all contrary actions against God; sin! God had to tell us indeed, what sin was!

It is not the other beast of the fields and or even the mega-beast in the midst of the oceans and the seas that we question whether or not Satan might have been present during their creation, but we often ponder over whether God allowed Satan access to our moment of creation; as if God feared that Satan could have made a difference or even stopped God from creating us in His own Image and Likeness.

Can't you even imagine that Adam must have walked around feeling disgusted and devastated over the displacement of himself and his wife, after only what seemed like a small little deed, after all it was only once that he had partaken of the fruit of the tree? Though it was not at all innocent, God had thoroughly warned him! Adam had been faithful being like God in the earth clear up unto the point to which he actually chose to listen to another voice other than the voice to which he had been in covenant with.

Sin humiliated Adam and had him feeling very silly and possibly even stupid and now empty as a man having to realize that the voice of God had never lead him to such low levels of living without the presence of God.

Whenever Adam communicated with God in the garden it made him to feel stronger and even more secure having been so much like God from creation now formed as a man in the earth.

The greater mystery in the garden is revealed when we determine to look just a little deeper into the spirit of God, according to the written word of God, we realize that God; totally released Himself into man from the beginning of creation, whereas no division could ever be allowed.

I asked the question; "why is it that Satan went after mankind to cause them to be separated from God even as he himself has been permanently separated eternally?" Many people still don't quite understand why it is that Satan doesn't like

mankind, and why it is that Satan has sought to destroy man since from the beginning of time. What is it about mankind that unsettles Satan to the point that he tries to destroy every trace of a possible relationship between man and God? Hmmm! I'm glad you asked...............

Adam did not even have a need for peace because of the total assurance that he pleased God daily! The God in Adam knew how to please God in Heaven on the throne! The God in Jesus Christ said to the Jews, *"and He that sent me is with me: the Father has not left me alone; for I do always those things that please him.* St. John 8:29 God always pleases God!

Adam and Jesus Christ are mirror images to each other, the differences being that one Adam was formed in the earth as a man sinless in the image and the likeness of God; and the other Jesus Christ came from the very presence of God as a babe in the womb of a mother in a prepared body in the same like human form of sinful flesh, but lived sinless successfully, even to the point of death, burial, and the resurrection.

Satan understood the mystery of God being in the earth, now living alive in man in the garden, and he knows when God is living alive in those of us today! In the garden Satan knew for sure that God is God; there is none like unto Him! But he also knows that God don't lie!   God said; *"Let us make man and make him in our image and in our likeness;"* and it was so! (Genesis 1:26)

God was as pleased with Adam even as He is pleased right now today with Jesus Christ!   God made man in His own image and likeness and it pleased Him, to the point that He knew that man was indeed just like Him!   Where we miss it all is not understanding that we were both created in the spirit; as God is a spirit and being created in the image of God means that we have the spiritual likeness of God; and we were formed in the natural from the dust of the earth as natural human beings. We are *Hue-Man* beings:

Hue -*a type or kind in a particular range; the way that something looks............*

God created us as man; but He formed us as Human; in the one man Adam every man woman boy and girl of every tongue nation skin color and geographical origination was also formed at the very instance.   Whereas God himself would only be multiplied as mankind would also multiply and be divided into the multi-diverse Hues of mankind, and Satan knew it!   The very moment that Adam was formed out of the dust of the earth, Satan was immediately outnumbered!   Perhaps with every diminutive grain of the dirt, or with every speck of dust, was the origination of every group of people over the entire face of the planet earth.

Satan; who was created as Lucifer, was never formed in the earth, nor created to live in space of time that we as humanity were created to live. His advantage of haven been blessed to look upon God; as God's own worshipper, had now become Satan's curse, in that he no longer would be accepted as a true worshipper to God; he knew the beauty of God; therefore he was familiar to the image of God, but to the form of man, Satan was totally in the dark and enraged that God would say that man was like Him. The pride in Satan would never allow him to see the true beauty in the human form of mankind, as we were not even as beautiful as he had been made in Heaven.

The purposeful devise of Satan's own scheme of sin was to show God just exactly how unlike God the newly formed worshippers were! Satan chose to try and to convince God that the formed man would be more like him than he would ever be like God in that they had the propensity to sin! Satan created sin and swiftly found out that God rejected it, with extreme penalties. Satan knows that God don't sin, and he knows that those who are truly transformed by God in the renewing in the spirit of their minds, putting us back into the remembrance of our spiritually originated image and likeness to our Father which has never changed, that we don't purposefully indulge ourselves in sin.

Without a doubt, Satan knew that Adam believed what God said about him as a man, in that he was proud, thankful and worshipful to be just like God. As a matter of the fact as Satan observed Adam in the garden, he realized that Adam behaved himself just like his Father did in Heaven.

Only, the confusing thing to Satan was the purpose of Adam doing so in the new domain of the earth in the garden. God had forever put Satan in remembrance of the beauty of Heaven, which would be an unrelenting pain in the spirit of Satan. He longs forever to be returned to the fellowship of Heaven with the Father to be again accounted as one of His own, but that is forever impossible for Satan, his punishment is set!

Haven been in heaven since before the beginning of the creation of the earth, Satan was familiar to the Heavenly atmospheric condition in which was now in the earth; which displeased Satan knowing that he would never be able to take

part in any portion of Heaven's activity ever again!

God never hid Satan behind a veil or some sort of a cover to disclose the works of His own hands whenever he began creating man and devising our purpose in the earth as the new worshippers. And neither was God concerned that Satan would visit the garden domain to shake up the peaceful fellowship of the most wonderful creation of the natural realm of existence, since Satan had been locked away from Eternal Life, now being sentenced to Eternal Death! Whatever God does in Heaven he can also do in the earth at will; Satan is not like God, he has not been given the precedence to do all over again what was indeed done in Heaven.

Satan looked upon the man and decided in jealousy that the man should fall away from the pleasure of pleasing God even as he had fallen away, eternally.

Here in is where we arrive back to the point in fact of a forbidden tree in the midst of the garden, whereas Satan who knows God for sure, knows that God means whatever he says the moment that He says it.

Satan heard God's instruction to Adam, but he also knew what was indeed hidden into the fibers of the tree. Satan knew that one bite of the fruit from that tree would begin a never ending chase for all humanity. Human existence would forever be founded upon a fallen nature.

That which gives us the true assurance that we have actually exited the fall of man as a sinner and have come back into fellowship with God is the total peace that we now experience since haven been afraid of the impending punishment of eternal destruction with Satan and all of the fallen host of the angels for haven been a sinner without the forgiveness of our sins, through the shed blood of Jesus Christ.

As mankind we don't mind sinning with Satan, but as many have been deceived to believe, most people don't feel that God who is love would allow us to suffer the same penalty of hell with Satan, or at least we foolishly continue to hope against the infallably written word of God. God loves sinners, but there is not one sin, nor unrepented sinner that will ever enter heaven! God loves you; God is Love!

God loved Lucifer in Heaven to the point that He separated Himself from all that is corruption and destruction the instance it was revealed and found in Lucifer. Thank God that He is not like man, in that we have a hard time separating ourselves from that which has the ability to destroy us, especially when that something happens to be someone!

We say often because we love someone, that just because they are on a very destructive downward spiral that we should go down with them and not to abandon them. That's crazy! Just because you make it impossible for me to live with you because of your destructive behavior, doesn't mean that I should also die with you! That's stupid! See you on the other side...............................

All along we have ridden the backs of Adam and Eve for the fall back in the garden, because of sin when it is actually the backs of Satan and the third part of the fallen host of heaven that has caused the separation and the pains of humanity as a result. I hear more people making excuses for what is actually sin, arguing with other leaders in the body of Christ about what qualifies a thing to be called a sin and why they don't think that it is or could ever be a sin!

Sin was at that time as new to Adam and Eve as the Noon-Day sun and everything else that existed in the garden. Take into consideration the fact that sin was not a common thing in the garden. It had not yet been given to mankind the need to examine excitement and the culprit responsible for bringing the excitement. The real focuses that we have missed all along in the plight of mankind are the unsought out explanations in the wake of Satan and his sneaky little scheme called sin, usually the direct result of not haven asked any questions that would lead us to revelations from God that would give us the true understanding!

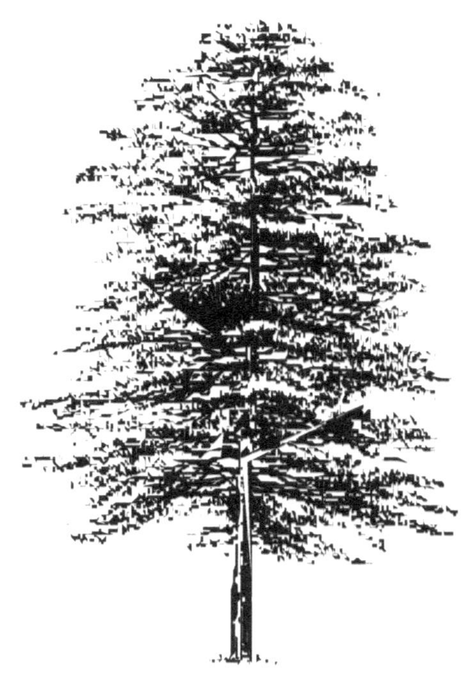

The Lasting Bite Marks***

for the children of this world are in their generations wiser than the children of light. St. Luke 16: 8b

Many of the people who have come into the church to stay, have further determined that they are going to stay away from the ultimate relationship with God so as to be sure not to anger or even to stir the attention of Satan.

It is those who have purposed to have a right relationship with God that Satan cites as worthy opponents for spiritual warfare. The closer that we as the children of the body of Christ get to the Lord through the word of God and prayer, living accordingly to the plan of God's intended purpose for our lives, Satan intensifies the warfare against us for a truth.

Close to God is where Satan resided as an Archangel in Heaven being the chief worshipper, there was none like Lucifer mainly relative to his anointed purpose for being made so excellent and beautiful. Understand that Lucifer was and is not the only beautiful angelic being ever created in Heaven, there is indescribable beauty in Heaven that we would never even be able to fathom with

181

the human minds that we have now, even as brilliant as many of our minds are, until we make it to Heaven to see it for ourselves haven been changed from mortal to immortal beings; from human beings to spirit beings forever.

I think that most true believers can attest that Satan is angry with all believers for sure. They just don't seem to have a truthful grasp on why it is that he would have been so angry with the people of the churches for being saved set free and delivered, to the fullest.

Someone along the way chose to create their own solutions for dealing with Satan, which they chose to just stay out of the way of Satan.

Well; Too Late! The only reason that people have not gotten saved set free and delivered is all because of the subtle deception of Satan who has blinded the minds of those who cannot see the cause of their determination to reject Jesus Christ.

Staying away from the spirit of the Lord doesn't guarantee that you as a human being will be totally secured from the destructive interest of Satan, and neither does it put you out of Satan's direct path, but it does place you inside of his reach.

Being saved alone is not what angers Satan to the point that he launches an attack against your life. In the eyes of Satan you are already guilty of being a potential threat simply because you are a human being but created in the image and the likeness of God. Satan knew what God was building whenever He began to work on the form of mankind from the dust of the earth, to place him in the earth's realm to have dominion in the earth.

Too often the people of the churches have been allowed to underestimate the true power of God, in that they are consistently thinking that God is somewhat worried or concerned about Satan and what it is that he just might be doing in the earth. If such were the case God would have stepped into the garden after the fall of mankind in search of Satan.

However, God never called for the whereabouts of Satan because He already knew where Satan was, and He knew what the devil had done to the once anointed realm of humanity destroying the even flow of the spirit of God in the earth's atmosphere between God and man.

God also knew that mankind had been lied to and that they would be forever seeking to find the truth in the midst of the lies that Satan had told them, of which no truth can ever be found in the midst of lies other than the fact that the lies are truly lies for a truth! In the garden of Eden Satan and the serpent caused the focus of man to be out of whack, whereas man would begin to look to knowledge and scientific explanations, even to other mere men seeking to find the opening to restore the relationship with God that we once had.

Science only makes discoveries based on that which is already here on the earth and in the earth's atmosphere, but, God created everything that is available to be discovered. Science can't box with God!

Man has been on a quest to find God who has never been lost or displaced from humanity, just separated from any common fellowship with man as there is nothing common about God at all. We really do want God and all that He has to offer to humanity, only we have our own agendas attached to our desire to be close to Him now.

God wants us to be close to him, but without a doubt God wants us close according to the purpose of which had been established before the foundation of the world. God don't make deals and for certain he does not allow created human beings to push Him around and tell Him what to do for us.

The Father knoweth what things that we have need of even before we take the time to ask for those things. But He knows whether or not we are actually ready to have those things, and whether or not we would even give Him the glory for those things being given to us. It's God's delight to give good gifts to them that ask of Him in Jesus name.

Only we as people are often found to be living with guilt as result of sin and shame. Guilt conditions our minds to think that God would not desire to bless us which is wrong. God desires to bless us always but our guilt and our shame will have often blocked the hands of God and stopped the blessings from getting to us.

God had given Job everything that a man on the face of the earth could ever think of; the more Job showed his faithfulness to God, God blessed him. It's God's desire that we who are His people, that we would have the very best of things and not just what's left of the rest of things only after everything has been through the hands of the sinners and the ungodly.

Evil knowledge has gotten the people of the body of Christ thinking that we are to show up before God looking like we had just gotten out of a battle with a lion, ragged and torn, bleeding profusely and financially embarrassed before the rest of the world, as if to suggest that God don't care for His own! God Cares; For His Own!

Satan's attack on Job the most upright man in the land of Uz, was an attempt to remind God of the former and the past bite marks back in the garden, suggesting to God that Job couldn't be that much more honest and true than that of Adam, after all it was Adam who was just like Jesus; yet he was able to turn the stomach of Adam in the garden and cause him to crave for that which was forbidden; Adam eventually sold out humanity for just one bite.

But God in the face of bitten, smitten humanity had a surprise for Satan, He testified for Job! God told Satan that Job would stand and never waver. Whatever God Says Is Always Right! And He's Right The First Time!

Whenever we read the story of the attack of Job in the bible we become aware that Satan touched Job's body to the point in fact that there were sore boils all over his body. The bible states that the flesh fell from his bones, no doubt metaphorically indicating the process of the rapid weight loss from being so sick?

The picture comes in a little clearer of the serious jealous anger and the rage of Satan over

the formed human body. Satan made it to appear as if this supernaturally abundantly blessed man of God, Job; as if he had sinned against God thus bringing down the penalty for sin behavior.

Sin when it has finished with you, it opens the door to multiple sicknesses and renders you vulnerable to the attachment of sickness and disease, thus finally unleashing the ultimate penalty for sin upon your body which is death. (James 1: 15)

Sin also has the ability to weaken you spiritually to the point of changing your position on God, which is the reason that God ask; "Adam where are you?" Have you stopped believing me? Have you decided that you don't want to be like me any longer now that you know how to think for yourself?

Do you have any idea of how many sins there are in the world, and if so could you possibly name them all; are you that close with Satan that he has revealed his secret arsenal to you in totality? I am of the opinion that the only way to know of every type of sin there is in the world is to know the devil personally.

Like it or leave it, God's purposes for you are not to teach you all of the sins and the recognition of such, but rather His purpose is to show you God and the inner workings of the Kingdom of God in the earth. You need to know the true power of the anointing and not the generic religious version of the anointing that is attached to everything in the world!

The half steppers in the churches are always classifying things as sins that are not sins because they are still attached to passive sinning in secret and the devil attached to sin wants everyone else to be guilty of sin as well.

Information will teach you the knowledge of sin, but it takes revelation to teach you the power of living Holy through the written word of God, leading you to the deeper insights of God's purposes for the body of Christ in the earth, so that you will never feel that you are just a mere human being with no spiritual authority to put the devil in his place.

Even Job's closest friends came along accusing Job of having sinned, because there was just no way that a man could be caused to suffer in his body like that, they thought anyway, except for in the presence of sin being attached to his life.

They knew that God hated sin just that bad! The word of God to the generations prior to the coming of our Lord and savior Jesus Christ was blatant and to the point without mercy for sinners, even to the priest! Many people dropped dead on the spot in the light of sinning against God intentionally! It pleases Satan every time he sees a body put to death and cut short of living because of Sins.

Satan is a formless spiritual being; he has never had a body of his own; this is the reason that he is always attacking the bodies of people all over the earth in every country and on every continent.

It is a shame that Satan has a better since of knowledge more than the average human being, of the privilege that we have been given which is the unique upright forms of our human bodies.

If Satan could have the benefit of being able to live in your body, he would kill you in a heartbeat just to have your body for his own. God never intended for Satan to have a human form, as Satan is not a man, he is a spiritual being, though formless and without a shape to be called his own.

While Adam took his first bite of the forbidden fruit, Satan was simultaneously taking his initial bite into the nature of our humanity also. All truth is parallel; we know that in the mouths of human beings there is saliva which has been found to be highly infectious upon biting which breaks the skin of another individual, however the infectious dribble flowing from the mouth of Satan was indeed sin!

Satan's bite was indeed more deadly than that of the serpent in that Satan's successful kill is eternal.

The snake could bite you and kill you as a result of the poison, but as sure as you have been saved sanctified and filled with the Holy Ghost, you will live forever in the presences of God; wherever God lives you will live there too! The snake's bite injects venom into the bloodstream of its victims; however Satan's bite injects demons into the spirit of his victims.

Humanity has definitely been sickened ever since being bitten back in the garden, whereas Jesus came as the antidote to the spiritual sickness of mankind. He came as the balm in Gilead to heal the sin sick souls of mankind!

Even the physical sickness which will eventually take hold of all mankind as a result of living a sinful life, Jesus took 39 stripes on His back on the way to the cross of Calvary to heal all of humanity that would believe on Him with their hearts, and confess Him with their mouths.

By His stripes we are healed! And with His stripes we are healed!

However, not all people are willing to come to Jesus to receive His sacrifice for their sins to be saved and healed and washed in the precious blood of the Lamb of God.

The infectious injection into the spirit of humanity has long since taken the negatively adverse effect on humanity whereas mankind has been moving further and further away from the principles of God. As of late over 50% of humanity is now living spiritually unconscious, they are on spiritual life support hanging on for dear life, suffering the possibilities of eternal damnation at any moment.

Spiritually we are suffering heart trouble, whereas the sinful attack on humanity has gone right to the heart of all humanity which is the family! Family life in our world is definitely sick and under major attack. If we don't be healed soon, death is for certain!

It wasn't until after Adam and Eve sinned in the garden after that they realized that they were naked that they came together sexually and began to reproduce to replenish the earth and to multiply humanity.

It wasn't really long before the hidden strike

of knowledge was spewed into the minds of mere men, whereas they became aware that they could perform the same sexual behavior between themselves male and female without being married, but only without the blessing of the Lord, and most people have never even cared that they lacked the blessing of the Lord, which also meant that they were in sin.

Being left alone in sin without the savior, the idealistic fantasies of man have progressed to such a selfishly evil rage that the rottenness of the stinking thinking of mankind began to stink in the nostrils of God.

The sexual stinking thinking of humanity has bread a since of spiritual gangrene into the very idea of marriage and the family; whereas people are living out loud as a couple having never taking the marriage vows in commitment to each other, not even in practice.

Satan being a spirit being, he does not have the same ability as that of humanity, he cannot reproduce after his own kind, as a result he doesn't want us to reproduce after our own kind either, but it's our God given right and privilege, as well as our commandment from God to do so!

Satan has been twisting the minds of men and women ever since they were sent away from

the garden where they had been closest to the presence of God. According to the scriptoral accounts of Sodom and Gomorrah, men were influenced to turn their sexual desires onto their own same sexual genders.

We now refer to it as homosexuality and lesbianism, but Satan called it the destruction of the human race! All he needed was for humanity as a whole to agree with his agenda and to abandon God's agenda; he knows that no two men or two women could come together sexually and produce children between the two bodies of the same sex.

Satan knows that he could never undo what God the Father and Creator had done from the beginning of the Creation, be he became a master at deceiving the minds of selfish men and women, causing them to believe that God had perhaps made mistakes with their bodies, placing their spirits within the wrong genders! Liar!

Satan can't reproduce a natural form because he has no physical body to do so and neither does he have a comparable mate after his own kind, so he doesn't want you to do it right or even at all, even though we do have the ability to reproduce after our own human likeness!

Vast percentages of humanity have bought

193

into Satan's agenda and have accepted the wrong ideology of sex, love and companionship in every facet as being the right frontal capacity of living as a couple and a family unit.

Many people now feel that it is okay to hurry out to seek abortion clinics to rid them of what has been cited as unwanted pregnancies. There are so many things that are foul relating to abortions; many people are not even looking at the fact that the baby that has been aborted was also aborted with its purpose to humanity. Looking deeply into the annihilating scheme of abortion again you could see the extinction of the human race if everybody were to latch on to the idea as acceptable.

The iniquitous marriage of the gay lifestyle and abortion will definitely diminish the human population all over the face of the earth, especially at the alarming rate in which people are forgetting about God! Over the entire face of the planet, people want the sex every way that they can get it, but they don't want the results that come with sexual behavior.

There are perhaps many things that would have been changed in the realm of humanity had the person's chosen to change them, had they not been aborted.

We are finally to the point in time of celebrating the contributions of many of the past patriarchs and their gifts to the human welfare of all mankind alike. At all historical aspects of our society there are many names to be called from the past whereas we would all agree to the accolades given to each notable contrive.

It is electrifying to realize that they all were people whose mothers and fathers were responsible to bring forth the fruit of their own sexual contact, whether they were married and honorable in their own family reproduction, or should they had been in the wrong having sex outside of marriage.

You know as I do myself that people have devised all sorts of ways to have sexual relations; with animals, same sex, with children, and most desperately with themselves; A-sexual! God intended for sex to shared between a husband and a wife, it was never intended that an individual would start all by themselves as if to be practicing just in case.

Can't you see Satan in self-sex? One has to be consumed in the burning passion of lust, lasciviousness, and evil concupiscence; which is the lowest level of sexual deviance that drives an individual to explore the most grotesque levels of sexual filth and ungodliness.

People are more so entertaining the ideas of cyber-sex involving computer animation and other electronic machine apparatuses. That's crazy! While all of these ridiculous things are taking place simply because people are burning in their own lust, the stupidity of mankind suggests that we just live; and let live!

Satan has used sex over and over again to silence the pulpits of the churches, whereas the messages are desperately needed in the pulpits now to an even greater proportion than it may be needed in the pews.

It is very difficult to rebuke that to which you yourself are a part of, and blatantly guilty of in the present of the same people that is living the same sexually sinful lifestyles that your message is targeting!

Now that we know how to do that which is indeed evil and sinful among ourselves as human beings, covering ourselves in the habitual lifestyles of iniquity, Satan would now more than ever like to convince all people everywhere that there is no such real thing as living holy to the point of truly pleasing God.

The true deception is found within the mindset of the more common interest of our

society; people think that if the people that know God can't live clean and holy, there is no use in trying to come clean! I might as well live the way that I choose to do so and take my chances when I'm dead and gone! Maybe Hell Isn't Real After All!

We know a lot of things now; but we still struggle with knowing how to please God!